Zoey Lyndon's Crush Chronicles

Michele,
Thanks for your support!

Zoey Lyndon's Crush Chronicles
Copyright © 2023 by Micheal Anderson
All rights reserved.

No portion of this book may be reproduced, stored in a retrieval system, or transmitted in any form by any means—electronic, mechanical, photocopy, recording, or other except for brief quotations in printed reviews, without prior permission of the author.

First Edition
Printed in the United States

Library of Congress Control Number: 2023921342

ISBN: 978-1-7366167-6-5 (paperback)
ISBN: 978-1-7366167-8-9 (eBook)
ISBN: 978-1-7366167-7-2 (hardback)

Illustrations by Lara Calleja
Edited by Jessica Renwick

Published by:
JOA Press
Seminole, FL

Chapter 1

Growing Pains

Zoey glanced at her bestie, Tommi, while she hung her coat on a hook in her locker. Tommi looked at her eagerly, practically bouncing on her toes.

"Did you get my text this morning? I'd hoped we'd get a snow day!"

Zoey put away her lunch bag before slamming the locker door. "Yeah, I got it. When I woke up and saw it snowed last night, I thought for sure they'd call off school."

Since Tommi already put her things in her locker, the girls headed to class. The fifth-grade classrooms were located in the same hallway, and only fifth graders were assigned lockers. The hallway bulletin boards were decorated in various shades of pink and red with a Valentine's Day theme.

When they entered their classroom, Mr. Washburn, their fifth-grade teacher, had already started the lesson. "Find your seats and pull out your social studies books." As the girls took their seats, he walked to the front of the room and sat on the wooden stool next to the whiteboard. "I'm still missing a couple of permission slips. Remember if you don't hand in your forms, you won't be able to attend the trip to the State Capitol next week."

Zoey loved going on field trips and was looking forward to visiting the Capitol in Jefferson City. She turned in her permission form last week. Mr. Washburn wasn't nearly as fashionable as Mrs. P, Zoey's teacher from last year, but she thought his casual style of chinos and a fitted sweater suited him perfectly. You could tell he worked out because you could see his muscles through his shirts, and he always smelled nice too.

"Wassup Zoey?" Josh gave her a slight head nod.

"Oh, hey Josh!" Zoey opened her textbook to the chapter Mr. Washburn wrote on the board. "What's up with you?"

"Uh . . . uh . . . nothing," he stuttered.

Zoey glanced in the direction he was staring at to see if she could figure out why he appeared to be in a trance. But she didn't notice anything other than Tommi sharpening her pencil. *Hmpf, he must have been daydreaming.*

"We've been learning about the three different branches of government, and today we're going to identify the role of each branch." Mr. Washburn explained, "The Legislative Branch makes the laws, the Executive Branch carries out the laws, and the Judicial Branch evaluates laws."

Zoey thought it was interesting learning about the House of Representatives, the Senate, and Congress, and how laws were created then passed to the president for approval.

Mr. Washburn played a video about the Three Branches of Government and passed out a worksheet that asked students to match various roles to the correct branch of government.

Once the video ended, he instructed, "Put your books away and line up at the door."

Today was a C day and on C days Zoey had art class. Zoey stood behind Tommi as they walked around the corner to the fourth-grade hallway where the art class was. "We should be making our Valentine boxes today."

"Yeah, I know," Tommi replied.

When the class arrived at Ms. Warren's art room, she was placing supplies on the tables. "Good morning, students. Come on in, find your box, and take a seat."

Zoey quickly found her box and sat down to inspect it. When she was satisfied there were no dents, she placed it on the table. She noticed Grayson whisper something to Tommi while they were getting their boxes.

"Since Valentine's Day is Monday, you'll need to finish decorating your containers today," Ms. Warren said.

When Tommi sat down, Zoey leaned in and asked, "Why were you and Grayson all huddled up?"

"What're you talking about?" Tommi sounded confused.

"I saw you and Grayson whispering over by the window a minute ago. What did he want?"

"Oh, he wanted me to smell his breath." Tommi flicked her hand as if it was no big deal.

"Why?"

"I guess he wanted to know if it stank." Tommi avoided Zoey's eyes and focused her attention on inspecting her box.

Zoey pursed her lips and thought there was more to it but decided to let it go.

Josh—Zoey's boy bestie—and Grayson sat across from the girls.

Grayson cracked jokes as usual, thinking he was a comedian. "What's a three-letter word that starts with gas?" He asked with a goofy grin.

"Bruh! Here we go with another one of your corny jokes," Josh teased.

"C'mon, bro. You know my jokes ain't corny," Grayson said.

"Duh! Gas is a three-letter word," Josh replied.

"Nope. That's not it." Grayson snickered.

"Hmm . . . Is it gasket?" Tommi asked.

"What about gastro?" Zoey rubbed her chin.

"Nope! Those are more than three letters."

Josh glued light brown construction paper to the lid of his shoe box. "Bruh, just tell us already."

"It's car!" Grayson cracked up laughing.

Tommi chuckled. "That's a good one."

Josh smiled and nodded. "I'll have to remember that one."

Zoey agreed. Grayson could be pretty corny, but this was one of his better jokes. She continued to cut out purple and pink hearts of different sizes to decorate her box. She covered it in white construction paper and glued the little hearts all over it.

Tommi put the finishing touches of bright pink hearts on her Valentines box.

"That's nice!" Zoey told her.

"Thanks Zoey. I was hoping it wouldn't be too much with all the pink."

"No, not at all. Because you used like four different shades of pink, it looks good."

Josh and Grayson both made sports-themed boxes. Josh made his look like a basketball court with orange basketballs all over it. Grayson's was similar, except he drew a football field with a goal post and a football flying through it.

"Okay, class." Ms. Warren clapped her hands. "It's time to start cleaning up your tables and putting away your supplies."

"Dang, girl! You made a mess," Grayson teased, gesturing at the colorful scraps all over their table.

"Yeah! I know." Zoey admitted. "It looks like something exploded over here." She collected the paper scraps and returned her scissors to the supply container in the center of the table.

"Well at least your project turned out nice," Tommi said.

"Thanks, bestie. I think so too."

"Oh, I agree. It looks great Zoey," Grayson said with a devilish smirk. "But you're still messy."

Once the supplies were returned to their proper place and all the scraps of paper were thrown away, the students collected their newly decorated boxes and lined up at the door.

"You did a nice job decorating your box," Josh told Tommi as they headed back to their homeroom.

"Thanks, Josh. So did you." Tommi's voice softened, and she cracked a smile.

Zoey turned around so she could hear their conversation. When she turned back to face the front of the line, she thought about how both Josh and Grayson had taken an interest in Tommi lately. Tommi's such a tomboy, but she's also very pretty. Zoey thought the boys' interest could also have something to do with how her bestie blossomed over the summer. Zoey shrugged it off and walked back to Mr. Washburn's class.

During lunch, the fifth graders were allowed to sit wherever they wanted, which was nice since Emily and Olivia were in Mrs. P's classroom. Mrs. P had been their fourth-grade teacher, but this year she started teaching fifth grade. Emily and Olivia were so lucky to be back in her class again this year.

Zoey and Tommi were already seated at their usual table by the window overlooking the playground when Emily and Olivia joined them.

"Guess what!" Emily said excitedly as she set her tray on the table then sat down.

"What's up?" Zoey and Tommi asked.

"My mom said I can have a sleepover next weekend." Emily grinned.

"Sweet!" Zoey took a bite of her softshell taco.

"Count me in. We're about to be team no sleep," Tommi said.

"Who're you inviting?" Zoey asked.

"Well, of course you, Olivia, Tommi, and my cousin Jade."

"Oh, she's cool!" Zoey wiped some taco sauce from the corner of her mouth.

Olivia tugged at her shirt, revealing a strap on her shoulder beneath it. "Oh my God! I hate wearing this stupid thing."

"You'll get used to it after a while." Tommi laughed.

"Ugh! I don't think I'll ever get used to one of these." She continued to adjust her bra strap. "Zoey, you should be glad you're still flat chested."

Emily chuckled.

"What so funny?" Olivia asked.

"It's just that last year we couldn't wait to get boobs, and now that we have them, you don't want them."

Emily, Tommi, and Olivia laughed. Zoey didn't.

She thought back to last year. Trudy Jacobs had been the only girl in class with big boobs, and now practically every one of her friends had breasts. Except for her. She only wore a sports bra because all her friends wore them now. But the truth of the matter was if she didn't wear it, no one would notice. Her breasts were just beginning to sprout, whereas over the summer, Tommi and Olivia really blossomed. *Fortunately, Emily's weren't much bigger than Zoey's, but at least she wore a regular bra. And why the heck did Olivia throw Zoey under the bus like that? Not cool.*

"We finished our Valentine's boxes this morning," Zoey said, hoping to redirect the conversation.

"Sweet! I'll do mine this afternoon when I go to Ms. Warren's class. I already picked up my valentines." Emily took the last bite of her chicken sandwich.

"Oh, I wonder if anyone will get a special Valentine," Tommi teased.

Briar Ridge Elementary offered Cupid Grams as part of the fifth-grade student fundraiser. There was always an annual trip at the end of the school year for fifth graders. The Cupid Grams and Santa Grams were long stem foil covered chocolate roses which were sold as a way for students to raise money for their trip.

Emily blushed. "We'll just have to wait and see."

"Emily and Jacob kissing in a tree! K-I-S-S-I-N-G!" Olivia chanted.

"Shh!" Emily looked embarrassed and quickly

glanced around to see if anyone else had heard Olivia. "Be quiet! I don't even know if he likes me."

"Okay, okay! Sorry."

"We all know you'll probably get one from Jackson," Emily said.

Olivia always thought he was cute, but Jackson had hit a growth spurt last summer. Ever since school started this year, Olivia had been sweet on him. Right before the Christmas holiday, he worked up the courage to talk to her, and now they were always flirting.

The girls finished their lunch, cleaned off their table, said their goodbyes, and went to line up with their class.

Later that evening, Zoey and her sister Jasmine watched an episode of *The Wonder Years* once they completed their homework.

Their mom poked her head into the living room. "Girls, dinner will be ready in about fifteen minutes."

"Okay, Mom," Zoey replied.

"Oh, I used to love this show," the girl's mother admitted.

Jasmine looked over her shoulder at her mom. "This show is new. It just came out."

"I'm pretty sure that show came out when I was in middle school. They must've remade it," Mrs. Lyndon said before going back to the kitchen.

Jasmine had already been texting Aubrey and had her phone handy, so she googled it.

"Yep. Mom's right."

"When did it come out?" Zoey asked.

"1988."

"Wow! It's an old show." Zoey leaned back on the couch to watch the new version.

"Time to eat!" Zoey's mom called.

The girls went to the kitchen. Each of them scooped a small helping of fried potatoes and green beans onto their plates, then grabbed a baked pork chop. They poured themselves cold drinks and took their seats at the dinner table.

"When will Daddy be home?" Zoey asked, sprinkling a few drops of hot sauce on her pork chop.

"He'll be back on Friday."

Zoey's dad didn't have to travel often for work, but when he did, the house seemed quieter.

"So how was school today?" Zoey's mom asked before picking up a forkful of well-seasoned potatoes.

Jasmine was the first to speak up. "Mr. Day told me I'm playing first chair in the winter concert."

"That's impressive!" Mrs. Lyndon wiped her mouth with her napkin. "Your music teacher must think highly of you to promote you to first chair. Have you told your father yet?"

"Nope! Not yet. I want to surprise him. I was gonna wait until he got home."

"Congratulations, Jazz!" Zoey knew how hard her sister had been practicing her cello and was genuinely happy for her.

Jasmine leaned in and placed her elbows on the table. "Mr. Day couldn't believe how much my playing has improved, especially since I've only been playing for a year."

"I'm so proud of you, sweetie! Sounds like those private lessons and all your hard work are paying off." Mrs. Lyndon looked at Zoey and asked, "Anything exciting happen with you today?"

"I finished my Valentine's box, and it turned out really nice."

"Good. You completed it just in time."

"What's it look like?" Jasmine asked.

"It's white with pink and purple hearts. I took a picture, so I'll show you after dinner." Zoey pursed her lips together the way her mom did when she was irritated. "Do you know what Olivia had the audacity to say to me today?"

"What'd she say?" Her mom asked with a raised brow.

"That girl had the nerve to tell me I should be glad I'm flat chested," she said in a voice mimicking her friend.

"Hmm. Why'd she say that?"

"Ooh. Your girl is shady." Jasmine smirked.

"She made a big deal out of how uncomfortable her bra was, and how I should be glad I don't have boobs."

Zoey's mother placed her napkin on the table and paused for a moment. "I can tell Olivia's comment bothered you, and I'm sorry about that. But I'm sure it wasn't her intention to hurt your feelings. Zoey, everyone's body is different. Some of your friends will develop faster than you, and that's okay. Puberty is a process and the hormonal changes happening in your body aren't going to happen in the same timeframe as your friends."

Zoey looked down and moved the remaining potatoes on her plate with her fork. "I know, Mom. I didn't think she was trying to be mean, but it still made me mad."

Jasmine reached over and placed an index finger under Zoey's chin to raise her head. "Zo, you look fine! Don't ever let anyone make you feel like you don't measure up."

Zoey smiled and sat up straighter. "Thanks, Jazz!"

"Jasmine's right. You're perfect just the way you are, and we love you." Mrs. Lyndon got up from the table and carried her dishes to the sink. "Now, who's got clean up?"

The girls both knew it was a rhetorical question because most of the time it was their responsibility to clean the kitchen after dinner. Occasionally, their dad would do it to give the girls a break.

After the girls cleaned up, Zoey went to practice playing her keyboard. She started taking piano lessons over the summer. Her parents refused to buy her the piano she'd asked for, but they agreed to purchase her a keyboard. Her lessons were only once a week after school, but she hadn't been practicing like she was supposed to.

Zoey practiced playing the C major scale C, D, E, F, G, A, and B. She finished up with playing a version of *Twinkle Twinkle Little Star*. Tired of playing a baby song, she hoped her piano teacher Miss Michelle would give her a new one to start. Zoey continued to practice, but her thoughts drifted back to Olivia's snide comment: *You should be glad you're still flat chested.*

Chapter 2

Zoey Gets A New Look

The next morning when Zoey came down for breakfast, Jasmine was already eating a slice of toast with some apple jelly on it.

"Good morning, kiddo," Zoey's mom said as she sipped her rose and vanilla tea.

Zoey opened the pantry and pulled out a box of cereal. "Morning, Mom. Hey, Jazz."

"Zoey, it's too cold out for that summer shirt. Go upstairs and put on something more appropriate," her mother instructed.

"Okay. I'll do it after I eat."

"You'll do it now," her mother said in a no-nonsense tone.

"Ugh!" Zoey grumbled under her breath. "Okay." Zoey ran upstairs and changed into a purple fleece hoodie covered in white dragon flies and returned downstairs in a flash. Jasmine had already finished her breakfast and was getting ready to go to the bus stop since her school started earlier than Zoey's. Zoey liked being able to talk to Jasmine before school, but today she wasn't going to have time.

"Much better." Her mom approved the fleece selection over the short-sleeved shirt Zoey had been wearing earlier.

Zoey poured herself a bowl of cereal, added some milk, and quickly ate her breakfast. She checked her phone for messages. She and her friends had a group chat they used to text back and forth, but there weren't any new messages since last night. After Zoey rinsed out her bowl, she grabbed her lunch bag, puffy coat, and told her mom she was ready for school.

When Zoey arrived at school, she put her things in her locker and greeted a few of her classmates as she hung up her coat. After she entered her classroom, she found her seat and chatted with

Tommi while they waited for class to start. Mr. Washburn gave them a math quiz and a spelling test before lunch. At lunch, the girls met at their regular table.

"Oh my God! I can't believe how cold it is today," Tommi griped as she zipped her hoodie to her chin. She rubbed her hands together.

"I know. It's like they don't have the heat on today," Zoey said. She was grateful her mother made her change her shirt that morning.

"I didn't notice how cold it was earlier, but I can definitely tell the temperature has dropped since this morning." Olivia dipped a tator tot in her ketchup then popped it into her mouth.

Zoey agreed. "Yeah, it feels like it's colder now than this morning."

"So did anyone purchase a chocolate rose for that special someone?" Emily asked.

Students were given the opportunity to purchase a Cupid Gram prior to Valentine's Day to be delivered during homeroom period on Valentine's. Most people sent them to another student they liked, and sometimes they were sent anonymously.

"Not me. I didn't have anyone I wanted to send one to." Zoey took a bite of her turkey sandwich and glanced at her friends.

"Me either," Tommi said.

"I sent one to Jackson," Olivia gushed. "I guess we'll have to see if anyone sent us one."

The girls speculated about who might receive a Cupid Gram and talked about the field trip next week while they finished eating their lunch. Once lunch was over, they threw away their trash and lined up to return to class. That afternoon, Mr. Bradshaw, the school principal, dismissed school early due to an issue with the furnace.

"Can you believe the heat went out at school?" Zoey asked her mom as they entered the house through the garage.

"No, but I'm glad Mr. Bradshaw made the decision to send everyone home," her mom replied. "It's entirely too cold to have students in school with no heat."

"Do you think they didn't pay their bill, and

the gas company turned off the heat?"

Zoey's mom chuckled. "I'm sure they paid the bill, silly goose. But it looks like your school will be closed until Monday."

"Yasss!" Zoey gave a little victory fist bump. "Jasmine is going to be so jealous." She smiled and hung up her coat in the hall closet.

She smelled something good cooking. "What's for dinner?" She asked as she headed up the stairs to drop her backpack in her room.

"Chicken and noodles and cornbread," her mom yelled up the stairs.

Since Zoey had eaten lunch not too long ago, she wasn't hungry and decided she'd watch a little TV and wait for Jasmine to get home.

After watching a couple of shows, Zoey got up to make a few pizza bagels to hold her over until dinner. When she popped them in the microwave, Jasmine walked into the kitchen.

"Hey! What're you doing home?" Zoey set the microwave for 60 seconds. "We didn't have heat at school today, so they sent everyone home. And school's closed tomorrow too."

"Seriously?" Jasmine looked surprised. "You're

so lucky." She put away her coat, then returned to the kitchen. "Keep the bagels out please."

Zoey left them on the counter, then the timer dinged, and she carried her plate to the table.

"What time did you get home?" Jasmine asked as she arranged her pizza bagels onto her plate.

"Mom picked me up about an hour ago."

Jasmine sealed the bag closed and returned it to the freezer before placing her plate in the microwave. "So basically, tomorrow you have a free day."

"Yep!" Zoey grinned from ear to ear.

"So not fair!" Jasmine teased. The microwave dinged again, and she removed her plate from it, grabbed a napkin, and sat at the table with her sister.

"Anything exciting happen today?" Zoey asked.

"Nah, not really. Mr. Day told us we would have our stage rehearsal one day next week and our full-dress rehearsal the day before the concert."

"When's the show?"

"February twenty-third." Jasmine took another bite of her snack.

"Oh, that's coming up quick," Zoey replied, her

mind wandering. "Do you think Case will get you anything special for Valentine's Day?"

Zoey could see her sister's eyes light up the way they always did when she talked about her boyfriend.

"I don't know. Probably not. When you're in middle school, you don't pass out valentines like you do in elementary."

"Girl, you know you'll be mad if your boo don't get you a gift for Valentine's Day," Zoey teased.

Jasmine chuckled. "No, seriously, I don't know. I mean, it's not like I have ever had a boyfriend before, so I'm not sure about the whole boyfriend/girlfriend protocol for stuff like this."

"So did you get him something?"

"Nope!" She grinned.

"Well, I still need to make out my valentine cards. I don't think I'm going to give one to Trudy though." Trudy Jacobs was the class bully and used her size to intimidate other students. Ever since Zoey stood up to her last year at Josh's birthday party, they had somewhat of an understanding. Trudy no longer harasses Zoey and her friends the way she used to, but they're still not friends.

"Since you're home from school tomorrow, you definitely have time," Jasmine said. "And I don't blame you for not wanting to give ole sticky fingers Trudy anything. Anyway, I'm gonna get started on my homework because I want to practice my cello after dinner." Jasmine got up, pushed her chair in, and loaded her plate and cup into the dishwasher.

"Do you want to watch Shrek later?" Zoey asked.

"Sure."

Zoey headed up to her room and put away her school things. She decided she'd address her valentine cards now to get it out of the way.

Mr. Washburn had given everyone a list of all the students in their class. Zoey pulled it out of her backpack and started addressing the envelopes with each student's name. She made out one for Trudy even though she wasn't sure if she'd give it to her. Zoey acknowledged Trudy was not as bad as she was last year, but she could still be pretty nasty at times.

When Zoey finished labeling the cards, she thought about practicing the piano. But she got sidetracked from a text from her bestie.

TOMMI: "how r u enjoying ur no heat day?"

ZOEY: "Lol love it! wht r u doing?"

TOMMI: "mom's getting ready to wash my hair"

ZOEY: 😬 "wash days r the worst"

TOMMI: "she's gonna blow out my hair so it'll b straight. u should have ur mom straighten ur hair 2"

ZOEY: "um . . . prolly. i'll ask her"

TOMMI: "Ttyl"

ZOEY: "K byee"

That evening after dinner, Zoey and Jasmine watched Shrek before getting ready for bed.

Zoey was excited to sleep in the next morning since school had been cancelled. She didn't get to see Jasmine before she headed out, but it felt good to have a lazy day. After making her bed, she put on a hoodie and a pair of leggings, then went to see what her mom was up to.

Zoey found her in her office seated at her desk. "Good morning, sleepy head," she said.

"Morning, Mommy." Zoey plopped down in the chair in front of the desk and propped her feet up on the matching ottoman. "What're you working on?"

"Just finishing up a piece for a business journal." Her mom smiled. "You hungry?"

"Yes."

"There's a few slices of bacon on the kitchen counter, or you can make a waffle."

Zoey stood and headed toward the door. "Okay. Hey, do you think you could straighten my hair?"

Mrs. Lyndon looked surprised. "Why do you want your hair straightened?"

"Tommi said her mom is going to blow out her hair and asked if I could wear mine straight too."

"I'll have to wash it first." Her mom's fingers

tapped the keys on her laptop. "How about we do it after you eat since I'm almost done here?"

Zoey grinned. "Let me know when you're ready." She went to get some breakfast.

After Zoey finished eating, she went upstairs to her mom's bathroom to get the shampoo, conditioner, and a towel, then took the items to the kitchen.

"Mom! I'm ready for you to wash my hair," she called.

A few moments later, her mom entered the kitchen. "Did you get the shampoo and conditioner?"

"Yes." Zoey nodded her head and pointed at the items she'd placed next to the sink.

Her mom walked to the counter and examined the supplies. "Run back upstairs and grab a washcloth to cover your eyes with."

"Why do I need a washcloth? Don't you want me to lay on the counter like I normally do?"

"No, you're too big for that now. Today I'm going to have you stand and lean over the sink. But you'll need to cover your eyes with the cloth to keep the soapy water out of them."

"I'd rather just lay on the counter. I don't mind."

Her mom gave her a stern look. "Well, I do! So go upstairs and get a washcloth."

"Ugh." Zoey mumbled and did as she was told.

A few moments later, she took her position and stood on her tiptoes, leaning her head over the sink.

Her mom ran warm water over Zoey's wavy mane. "How's that feel?"

Zoey gave her a thumbs up. The water was going into her ears and nose, and she thought she might drown if she tried to speak. She held the rag to her eyes for dear life.

"Zoey, I'm going to need you to come closer to the sink or my floor will be soaking wet," her mom told her as she nudged Zoey closer.

Risking choking to death, Zoey said, "Okay." She took a step forward and stretched her neck even further under the cascading water of the faucet.

After her mom lathered her hair and rinsed it several times, she massaged in the conditioner which smelled of apricots and made her scalp feel tingly.

"I'm going to rinse you once more, and then we'll be done."

That was music to Zoey's ears. She gave her mom a thumbs up and kept her eyes covered.

"Okay! We're all done." Zoey's mom said as she wrapped a towel around her hair. "Have a seat at the table. I'm going to get the blow dryer and my oils."

"Okay," Zoey replied as she tilted her head to the left and then to the right to make the water slide out of her ears.

A few minutes later, Zoey's mom returned, ready to finish Zoey's hair. She removed the towel from Zoey's head and placed it on the table, then placed a fresh towel around Zoey's shoulders. Mrs. Lyndon parted small sections of hair at a time before combing through it with the blow dryer. She continued to work one section at a time before moving on to the next step. Once Mrs. Lyndon was satisfied her hair was dry and didn't feel any dampness, she unplugged the blow dryer.

"You can take a short break; I need to check my messages." Her mother picked up her cell phone from the counter and left the kitchen.

Grateful for the opportunity to stretch her legs, Zoey went to the bathroom to check her mom's progress, grabbing a couple of cookies from the pantry on her way. Once in the bathroom, she ran her fingers through her hair and loved how easily they glided through it. Normally, Zoey's hair was soft puffy curls that were hard to control, but now she couldn't get over how smooth it felt. She kept flipping her hair to the left and right.

A few moments later, her mom returned. "You ready to finish up?"

"Yes!" Zoey answered and finished off her second cookie. "Oh my God! This is taking forever."

"I know, sweetie, but straightening your hair will go a lot faster."

"I hope so," Zoey mumbled.

"You should be glad I don't have to use the hot comb. When I was younger, Nana Joyce would have me sit on the kitchen floor while she sat in the chair behind me and pressed my hair."

Mrs. Lyndon parted another section of Zoey's hair. "And I dreaded getting my edges done because if I didn't sit still or hold my ear down, you better believe I'd get burnt. And your grandma would swear it was because I moved." She belted out a laugh. "Lord! I don't miss those days."

Zoey sat still because she didn't want to feel the heat from the flat iron. She was glad her mom never used a hot comb on her.

Almost thirty minutes later, her mom unplugged the flat iron and laid it on a dry hand towel.

"All done," she said, tapping Zoey on the shoulders. "Do you want to go take a look?"

"Yep." Zoey sprung to her feet and went to check out her hair in the powder room.

Her face lit up when she saw how long her hair was and how it seemed to cascade past her bra strap. She ran her fingers through it and smiled from ear to ear. The oils her mom massaged through it gave it a nice shine and smelled wonderful. She couldn't believe how much bounce her hair had. Every time she turned her head, her hair moved effortlessly. Pleased with the outcome, she turned off the light switch and returned to the kitchen, where she could still hear her mother moving about.

"I love it!"

"Glad you approve," her mom chuckled. "You'll have to wrap it up at night if you want it to last."

"I know." Zoey knew her mom meant she would have to brush her hair around her head and tie it with a silk scarf to maintain the style. Jasmine sometimes wrapped her hair, and it always reminded Zoey of a big cone. She knew it worked, because whenever Jasmine did it, the style would last a long time.

Zoey's mom returned the shampoo, conditioner, and other items to her closet. Zoey decided to take a couple of selfies to send to Tommi.

Still wearing the hoodie and leggings from earlier, she decided to put on a pair of gold pear-shaped earrings and a little lip gloss before snapping the pictures. She added a few swipes of her sugar poppy gloss and smacked her lips together. She poked out her chest and looked at her reflection from the side to see how she looked. Clearly, nothing had changed in that area.

She resumed her normal posture and took in her appearance. Pleased with her reflection, she thought, *I look so different with my hair down. I hope the boys will notice me now, and maybe I'll get a secret admirer for Valentine's Day. It seems like everyone has someone interested in them, and it looks like Grayson and Josh might like Tommi.* Zoey wasn't jealous that the boys were starting to like her bestie, she just wanted someone to take an interest in her too.

Zoey snapped several pictures and texted a couple to Tommi, then went down to the family room to watch one of her shows.

Zoey was watching TV when her dad's voice came booming through the house.

"I'm home!"

Zoey hopped off the sofa and ran to greet him. She found him in the kitchen.

"DADDY!" She gave him a hug.

"Whoa! Who is this?" He teased.

Mrs. Lyndon chuckled as she entered the kitchen to welcome her husband. "Zoey asked me to straighten her hair."

"Well, you certainly look like a big girl." He gave her a wink and walked over to embrace his wife, giving her a quick kiss on the lips.

"Aren't you supposed to be in school?" He asked.

Zoey quickly explained the heating situation at school.

"Aren't you lucky? No school and it's the weekend," he said, moving to the hallway to hang up his coat in the closet.

"I know right," Zoey replied. "This is the life." She went back to finish watching her show in the family room.

Friday nights were family nights in the Lyndon household, which meant playing a game and ordering pizza. Tonight was no exception. Zoey's dad picked up two large pizzas from their favorite pizza place. One was half cheese and half pepperoni, and the other was half meat lovers and half veggie. Jasmine liked cheese, and sometimes she would eat a few bites of their mom's veggie pizza. Zoey liked pepperoni and sometimes cheese. No one liked meat lovers, except for their dad.

"David, I think there's something Jasmine wanted to tell you," Mrs. Lyndon said as she placed a couple of veggie slices on her plate.

"Is that right?" Dad cocked his head.

Jasmine held up a finger as she finished chewing her cheese pizza. "Oh yeah! Mr. Day, my music teacher, told me he wanted me to play first chair in our winter concert."

"Wow! That's wonderful news. I'm happy for you, baby." He beamed the way he always did when one of his girls made him proud.

"Thanks, Daddy!" Jasmine said. "I found out the other day, but I wanted to surprise you with the news."

"Well, it's a wonderful surprise. And I'm glad those cello lessons are paying off."

"Mom, do you think you can take me to the stationary store tomorrow?" Jasmine asked.

"Why do you need to go to the stationary store?" her mom asked with a raised brow.

"Since Monday is Valentine's Day, I wanted to buy Case a card, in case he got one for me."

"So, just to clarify, you want to get him a card, but you're not going to give it to him unless he gives you one first?" Her father asked.

"Uh . . . yeah!"

"That's my girl!" Her dad erupted in laughter.

After dinner, the family played Monopoly but ended the game early because Mr. Lyndon could hardly keep his eyes open. Jasmine and Zoey decided to play a couple of hands of UNO instead.

Chapter 3

Cupid's Arrow

On Monday morning, Zoey was excited to go to school because she couldn't wait to see if any of her friends would receive a Cupid Gram. Plus, she couldn't wait for everyone to see how cute she looked with her hair down.

Zoey was surprised by how pretty her tomboy bestie looked today. Gone were the high-top J's and hoodie Tommi normally wore, replaced with a blush pink sweater, dark wash jeans, and a cute pair of light pink Timbs.

"You look amazing! I love your hair!" Zoey ran her fingers through Tommi's silky straight hair before dropping her backpack on the floor so she could open her locker.

"Thanks, Zoey." Tommi blushed. "Your hair looks good too." She let her fingertips glide through her friend's hair. "And I had no idea your hair was so long."

"I know. Me either," Zoey giggled. "The shrinkage is real."

The girls finished putting away their coats and lunch totes and headed to class. When Zoey walked into Mr. Washburn's room, she swore it seemed like all the boys were staring at her and Tommi. She thought she looked cute this morning in her navy sweater with pink and white hearts, gold heart-shaped earrings, a pair of corduroy jeggings, and her sugar poppy lip gloss. She even caught Trudy staring, although she tried to play it off.

Mr. Washburn took attendance before jumping into the social studies lesson. "Since we're going to the State Capital this week, I want to review the Three Branches of Government to make sure you all have a clear understanding of what each branch is responsible for." He wrote Team B and Team G on the whiteboard.

"We're going to play a little game, and it will be boys against girls."

"Oh, yeah! The girls are about to get crushed!" Grayson bragged.

"Bet!" Josh agreed and slapped a high five with Grayson.

"You chumps better get prepared to taste defeat," Trudy huffed.

"You're going down!" Zoey teased Josh.

"Simmer down," Mr. Washburn warned. "I have several flashcards and will read a question from one of them. The first person to answer the question correctly will earn a point for their team. The only rule is that you must raise your hand and wait to be called on. If you blurt out an answer, it will not count." Mr. Washburn removed the flash cards from the box. "Are there any questions before we get started?"

The students were excited and ready to begin.

"The House of Representatives is under which branch of government?"

There was a chorus of "Oh! Oh!" and students obnoxiously waving raised hands.

"Looks like Trudi was first," Mr. Washburn said. "What's your answer?"

"The House of Representatives is part of the Legislative Branch," she replied.

"Correct," he wrote one check on the board under Team G.

"What Branch of Government is the Supreme Court?" he asked.

The energy and excitement of the students who were eager to be called filled the classroom.

"I see your hand Josh. What's your answer?"

"The Supreme Court is under the Judicial Branch of government," Josh replied.

"Correct," Mr. Washburn said and put a mark under Team B on the board.

After completing the Social Studies review, they did a science lesson and learned about the different types of energy. Mr. Washburn talked about how valuable solar, wind, and geothermal energy were because they were renewable energy forms.

There was a knock at the door.

Mr. Washburn went to see who it was. "Hello."

"Hi, Mr. Washburn. We're on the Student Council, and we have some Cupid Gram's for some of your students," Jackson said. Emily was with him. She smiled and waved at her friends.

"Tell me which students have a Cupid Gram, and I'll call on them to come get them," Mr. Washburn said.

Jackson showed him the list, and Mr. Washburn called the students whose names were listed.

The class sat anxiously to see which of their peers would get a Cupid Gram or secretly hoped they would receive one.

"Josh Hightower," Mr. Washburn called.

Josh casually strolled to the door and looked like he was trying to hold back a smile.

"Here you go!" Emily handed him a chocolate rose covered in shiny red foil. There was a small white card attached that had to be opened to see who your Cupid Gram was from.

Josh took his seat, and Zoey could have sworn he glanced at Tommi. It looked like something had passed between them, and she was certain she wasn't imagining it.

"Zoey Lyndon," Mr. Washburn called.

Zoey lost all train of thought, and her eyes

widened in shock. She stood to retrieve her rose and didn't even try to hide her excitement.

"Oh! I wonder who it's from," Emily teased. "And LOVE the hair!"

"Thank you." Zoey instinctively ran her fingers through her hair. "I'll tell you who it's from at lunch." Zoey giggled. "Oh, and I like your headband. It's cute."

Emily wore a thin pink and sparkly headband with two pink glittery hearts attached to tall slender springs that bounced when she moved.

"Thanks, Zoey. See you at lunch," Emily grinned.

"Tommi Mitchell," Mr. Washburn called out.

Zoey took her seat and was excited to see her bestie also receive a Cupid Gram.

Emily handed Tommi not one but two foil covered chocolate roses. "Oh! Looks like someone has a secret admirer."

Tommi was gushing. "I have no idea who they are from."

"We'll talk at lunch," Emily said.

Tommi walked back to her seat and shyly glanced at Josh. Zoey looked at Emily to see if she saw the look that passed between Josh and Tommi. Emily's surprised expression let Zoey know she witnessed it too.

Zoey returned to her seat and waited for Tommi to get back to her desk so they could open the cards attached to their Cupid Gram's together.

"Who's your secret admirer?" Grayson whispered, leaning over Zoey's shoulder.

"I have no idea." Zoey grinned and shrugged her shoulders.

"Well, open it up, and let's see."

Zoey turned in her seat to look at Grayson. "Why do you care?"

"I don't." He huffed and sat back in his seat.

Trudy laughed. "Aw. Did Zoey hurt your wittle feelings?"

"Forget you, Trudy!" Grayson snapped. "Nobody was even talking to you."

Zoey chuckled and opened her card when she saw Tommi opening hers.

Aw. It's from Emily! Zoey smiled to herself at how thoughtful her friend was.

"Mine is from Emily," Zoey said. "Who sent you yours?"

"Emily sent me one and the other is from a secret admirer." Tommi blushed.

Zoey leaned across the aisle and whispered. "Do you know who the secret admirer is?"

Tommi grinned from ear to ear and shook her head. "Nope!"

Both girls giggled and redirected their attention to Mr. Washburn, who had resumed the science lesson from earlier. Once he was done, he assigned them homework.

When their class was lining up to go to lunch, Zoey saw Grayson and Tommi huddled together again. When Josh joined them, Zoey could hear them talking about how cool her pink Timbs were and how they hadn't seen them in that color before. Tommi thanked him for the compliment and came to stand with Zoey, who was saving her a spot in line.

"Thanks, Zo!" Tommi said as she slid into line.

"No problem. What did Grayson—"

"Tommi! You need to move to the back of the line," Trudy interrupted from behind Zoey.

Tommi rolled her eyes.

"I know you heard me," Trudy huffed.

Zoey turned around. "Tommi was already standing here, and I was holding the spot for her."

"No, she wasn't, and you know it!"

Zoey knew Trudy was right. "Well, I already held the spot for her, so just let it go."

"You think you're so cute!"

"No, I don't."

"Yes, you do. Little Miss Itty Bitty Titty Committee."

"Why don't you just mind your own business?" Tommi snapped. "Just ignore her." She placed her hand on Zoeys shoulder. "She's just jealous."

Zoey was fuming and wondered who heard the last comment Trudy made. She looked back at Trudy, and the girl had a wicked smirk on her face. Zoey held her composure as best she could, flipping her hair over her shoulder.

"What were you saying about Grayson?" Tommi asked.

"Huh?" Zoey remembered, "Oh, I wanted to know what he had said to you when we were lining up."

"He told me he liked my boots," Tommi replied.

Zoey felt something touch her hair. She tried to

flick it away with her hand. A few seconds later, she felt it again and ran her fingers through her hair to get rid of whatever it was.

She felt it once more as they walked down the hall. This time, she caught a glance of Grayson pulling his hand back to his side. He reached around Trudy and another student to reach Zoey, but she busted him this time.

"What's your problem, boy?" she snapped and gave him a stank face.

"Girl! I'm just playing," he laughed.

When the students entered the cafeteria, a fishy smell wafted through the air. Today they were serving fish sticks, hotdogs, and tator tots. Zoey and Tommi joined Olivia and Emily who were already seated at their usual table.

"Guess who got two Cupid Grams today?" Zoey said and opened her lunch bag.

"I already know! Emily told me," Olivia replied.

"Okay. Okay." Tommi laughed. "Let me sit down first."

Emily dunked a tator tot in some ketchup. "So, who was the second Cupid Gram from?"

Blushing, Tommi leaned forward and placed

her elbow on the table. "A secret admirer."

"SHUT UP!" Olivia scooted to the edge of her seat.

"You've gotta have an idea who it is," Emily said, opening her chocolate milk.

"No. I don't know." Tommi giggled as she opened her bag of chips.

Zoey bit into her turkey and cheese sandwich and eyed her bestie suspiciously.

"What's that look about Zoey?" Olivia asked.

"I think I know who sent Tommi the other rose," she answered.

"Who do you think?" Emily asked.

"I'm just connecting the dots," Zoey said. "You guys aren't in class with us anymore and haven't seen the way Josh is always taking sneaky peeks at Tommi. And I think she is trying to look cute for a special someone today."

"That's not true, Zoey!" Tommi snapped.

"Wait a minute!" Emily leaned forward and rested her forearm on the table. "You think Josh likes Tommi?"

"Yeah, I do! And I think Tommi might like him too." Zoey smiled.

"I don't like Josh!" Tommi blurted.

"Tommi, you are my best friend, and Josh is a good guy. It's totally cool if you like him."

"But I don't like him."

Zoey and her friends looked at Tommi to assess what she said.

"Okay, then. Well, that means someone else has the hots for you," Zoey teased and bit a pretzel. *Maybe her secret admirer is Grayson. Lately, they are always whispering about something.* She glanced at Emily. "By the way, thank you Emily for sending me a Cupid Gram"

Tommi and Olivia also thanked Emily for her thoughtfulness.

"No problem. I thought it would be nice if we all got one." Emily popped another tator tot in her mouth.

"Did you get one from Jacob?" Zoey asked.

Emily and Olivia immediately frowned.

"No!" Emily answered.

"Apparently, he's dating Amanda Cox," Olivia said with disgust.

Zoey knew Amanda and thought she was a nice girl. "I'm sorry, Emily."

"It's okay. He's not that cute anyway," Emily shrugged. "Tommi's not the only one who got two Cupid Gram's today."

Olivia's smile let everyone know she was also the recipient of two chocolate roses.

"Was the second one from Jackson?" Zoey asked.

"Yes," Olivia gushed.

"Seems like things are getting serious between you two," Tommi said.

"Not really!" Olivia giggled. "It's just a little flirting."

"A little?" Emily teased. "You should see the two of them in class."

Olivia couldn't hold back her laugh. "I know, but it's just innocent flirting."

"If you say so," Emily chuckled.

The girls finished eating, Olivia and Emily threw away their trash, and Tommi and Zoey placed their empty containers into their lunch bags.

Zoey didn't mention to Emily and Olivia about her little tiff with Trudy before lunch, and she was glad Tommi didn't mention it either. She didn't want to hear Olivia acting like boobs weren't a big deal or how she should be glad she doesn't have any yet.

Later that afternoon, the students placed the Valentine's boxes they made on top of their desk. They passed out their cards, and a few students gave out snacks for their valentine. Some were small bags of pretzels, rice crispy treats, and candy. A couple of the PTO moms provided snacks for the entire class.

Zoey and her classmates sat at their desks opening their cards and enjoying the festivities. Mr. Washburn gave out their homework and had the class clean up their area before they were dismissed for the day.

Zoey went to get her coat from her locker and waved goodbye to Tommi. *Oh shoot, I forgot my backpack!* Zoey closed her locker door. She turned to run and get it, and almost ran straight into Grayson.

"Here you go." He handed her the backpack. "You left it on the floor by your desk."

"Cool—thanks." She took it and slung it over her shoulder, then headed for the car ride line.

"See ya tomorrow!" Grayson yelled.

Zoey threw her hand up, waved, and continued to head toward the exit.

Zoey was lying on her bed with her ankles crossed when she heard the garage door open. Seconds later, her dad's voice boomed throughout the house. "Babe! You got the house smelling good. What's for dinner?"

Zoey ran to the kitchen, just as Mrs. Lyndon told him what she was cooking. "Just some pork chops, roasted Brussel sprouts, and dirty rice."

"Mm, mm, mm. That sounds good to me," her dad said.

"Dinner's ready. Go and change out of your work clothes and then we can eat." Her mom stirred the rice once more.

"Alright, babe. I'll be right back." He climbed the stairs two at a time.

"TIME TO EAT!" Zoey's mom yelled.

Jasmine entered the kitchen. "Smells yummy!"

"Your father's home. He got in a little while

ago." Mrs. Lyndon said as she removed plates from the cabinet.

The girls grabbed silverware from the drawer and poured drinks for everyone before taking their seat at the table.

Mr. Lyndon returned, all washed up, and took his seat at the head of the table. "How are my two beautiful girls?"

Zoey scooped the dirty rice onto her plate. "Hey, Daddy." She smiled, then picked up a pork chop and placed it on her dish.

"I'm fine, Dad." Jasmine answered while she prepared her plate.

Mr. Lyndon took a bite of his fried pork chop and let out a little moan. "See, this is why I married your Momma."

"David, stop being silly." Mrs. Lyndon chuckled.

"Rachel, I'm serious. You remember when we first started dating and you used to bake me those chocolate chip cookies? Girl, I knew you was a keeper back then," He laughed and took another bite of his chop.

"Well, I'm glad you think I still got it."

"Oh, you still got it, alright. And I definitely still want it!" he winked.

"Ew!" Jasmine turned up her face at her parents' playfulness.

"We're trying to eat here!" Zoey's face matched her sister's.

"Jasmine, did you end up giving the card to Case?" her mom asked.

Jasmine seemed glad the conversation had taken a different direction. "Yes." Her face lit up. "He gave me a box of chocolates and a little pink bear keychain that I already put on my backpack. I was so glad I picked up a card."

"That was mighty nice of him." Her mom looked as if she approved. "Zoey, did you pass out all of your cards?"

"Yeah." Zoey knew she was really asking if she gave Trudy a card. Zoey made one out for her, but after she was acting like a crusty booger, she decided not to give it to her.

"I got a Cupid Gram today," she said.

"What's that?" her dad asked.

"It's a chocolate rose wrapped in pink and red

foil that's delivered to your homeroom. It's one of the fifth-grade fundraisers," Zoey explained.

"Oh! Do you have a secret admirer?" Jasmine teased.

"No, I don't. Emily sent all of us one. But Tommi apparently has a secret admirer."

"Really? Who does she think it is?" Jasmine asked before taking a sip of her cranberry juice.

"She said she doesn't know. I told her I thought it was Josh because I keep catching them making eyes at each other but acting like they're not."

"And what'd she say?"

Zoey finished chewing her vegetables before she answered. "She said she didn't think it was Josh and acted like she hadn't noticed him looking at her. I mean, it's totally cool if they like each other."

Jasmine shrugged her shoulders. "I guess time will tell if it's Josh or not."

"It could also be Grayson, because I've noticed the two of them huddled up a couple times, but I feel like she knows something. She wanted to wear her hair down today, out of the blue. At first, I thought it was a coincidence, but Tommi never wears her hair down. And on top of that, she wore lip gloss—I've never seen that girl wear lip gloss."

"You wore your hair down today and had on lip gloss. Does that mean you wanted to look cute for someone?" Zoey's mom asked.

"No! I only wore my hair down because Tommi asked me too, and I always wear lip gloss." Zoey was irritated with her mother's implication.

"Well, I have Valentines for all of my girls," Mr. Lyndon announced before stepping away from the table. "I need to get something out of my car."

A few moments later, he was back with two small flower arrangements and one large bouquet of flowers. "This is for you." He handed one of the small arrangements to Jasmine. "And this one's for you, baby girl." He turned and handed Zoey the other vase of flowers.

"Thank you, Daddy!" the girls responded in unison.

"And these are for my best girl." He handed his wife the large bouquet, then leaned in for a kiss.

"Thank you, David!" Mrs. Lyndon beamed. She stood and went to get a vase for her flowers.

"I've got clean up tonight." He winked at his girls and started to clear the table.

"Thanks, Daddy." The girls took their flowers to their rooms and were grateful not to have to clean the kitchen.

Chapter 4

Breaking The Code

The next morning, after Mr. Washburn took attendance, he unlocked the technology cabinet. "Row one, please come up and get your tablet." The students in the first row walked to the front of the room to retrieve their computers.

"Row two, you can come and get yours," he said once the first group of students had returned to their seats.

Once the remaining rows were called and everyone was seated and logged onto their tablets, Mr. Washburn asked, "Who knows what coding is?"

Several students raised their hands to answer the question.

Mr. Washburn saw Josh's hand was up and called on him to answer.

"Coding is when you program a computer," Josh replied.

"That's right!" Mr. Washburn said. "And what can you program a computer to do?"

Josh shrugged his shoulders. "I don't know."

Mr. Washburn saw Trudy's hand. "Yes, Trudy."

"You can program a computer to do a lot of different things. My aunt has a robotic vacuum, and she set it up to clean in any room she wants."

"That's correct! You can program a computer to do a variety of things." Mr. Washburn left a subtle trail of his spicy smelling cologne as he walked around the classroom. "Coding is a set of instructions created to tell a computer what actions to take. For example, if the programmer would like to use the up-arrow key to make a character jump, they'll insert instructions to allow that to occur. A computer doesn't have the capacity to think independently, so we use code, which tells the computer what to do. We use things built with code every day. Can anyone think of how we use code on a daily basis?"

"Video games," Grayson answered.

Zoey raised her hand and called out, "Our cell phones."

"You're both correct!" Mr. Washburn wrote their answers on the whiteboard along with a few additional ways we utilize coding programs. "Mobile apps, games, and websites are just some of the things we access daily that function because of coding programs." He sat on the wooden stool at the front of the room. "Today, you're going to learn how to code by creating your own game."

"Oh, yeah!" Josh turned and slapped a high five with Grayson.

"This is way better than those boring math games we usually play." Grayson couldn't hide his excitement.

Mr. Washburn explained what Block Based Coding was and how each block is preprogrammed with instructions. Multiple blocks can be used simply with the drag and drop method. There are specific blocks used for motion, sound, or to change the appearance or to create a different background. He connected his laptop to the projector and was able to demonstrate how to select a template for your game, and then used the blocks to make it functional.

"Now that you've seen how it works, you can select the type of game you'd like to create," he instructed.

"I'm using flying tacos in my game," Zoey said.

"Oh! Where'd you find the flying tacos?" Tommi asked, and Zoey showed her.

"Bruh! Check out the sports themed templates." Josh scrolled through the different blocks.

"Cool," Grayson replied.

Mr. Washburn walked up and down the aisles, stopping to help anyone who had questions.

After the students had time to get familiar with block coding, Mr. Washburn had them return the tablets to the technology cabinet.

"Since the coding activity ran a little longer than expected, I'm going to postpone our math quiz."

Cheers erupted throughout the class.

"Try to hold back your disappointment." Mr. Washburn laughed as he looked upon all the happy faces.

"Line up and get ready for gym," he instructed, then slid on some lip therapy and returned the tube to his pants pocket.

"Packers, make sure you take your lunches with you because we'll be going straight to lunch afterward."

Zoey and Tommi quickly retrieved their lunches from their lockers and fell in line.

Mr. Lockwood was their regular gym teacher, but he'd been out because his wife had a new baby. Miss Shellman was his substitute, and she was a lot more fun.

"Come on in." Miss Shellman waved the class into the gym and walked over to speak with Mr. Washburn.

"I'm going to need you to pair up today. Each boy needs to partner with a girl," she said.

Zoey walked over and grabbed Josh's hand. "You can be my partner." She smiled, then let go of him and shoved her hands in her pockets.

"I already partnered with Tommi," he said.

Zoey's eyes narrowed. "Why?"

"I didn't know you wanted to partner with Josh." Tommi looked at Josh first, then to Zoey.

"I don't know why not. I always partner with Josh, and you always partner with Grayson when we have to pair up with the boys."

Tommi clasped her hands together. "Well, you can have Josh as your partner if you want."

"Never mind now!" Zoey tried to hide her irritation.

Grayson came up behind Zoey and placed his hand on her shoulder. "I was gonna ask you if you wanted to partner with me, anyway," he gave her a boyish grin. "C'mon, you can be my partner."

Zoey stood silent for a moment. "Thanks!"

Trudy snickered. "Trouble in paradise, huh?"

Zoey rolled her eyes and ignored her.

Miss Shellman finished her conversation with Mr. Washburn then walked over to the stage.

"You'll need to form three groups with four couples in each, then stand in the form of a square." She scrolled through the playlist on her phone and saw that the groups were in position. "This will be considered your home position." Looking at the only group missing a person, she nodded. "I'll dance with the third group, since you're missing a partner."

There were only two boys in the last group because our class had a lot more girls than boys.

Miss Shellman played some catchy upbeat country western song and put it on repeat, then joined the third circle.

"Today, we're going to learn how to square dance."

"Aw man! This is so corny!" Grayson mumbled.

A few of the other boys made faces and acted like they didn't want to participate.

After a while, Grayson started bobbing his head and stuck his thumbs through his belt loops, goofing off.

Zoey caught herself beginning to tap her foot to the beat of the music.

"Here are the basic steps you'll need to know." Miss Shellman called out each step and demonstrated.

"Circle left." All dancers in the circle clasped hands and walked left.

"Do-si-do." The students had to circle one another back-to-back.

"Swing your partner." The boys and girls had to place one arm around the waist of their partner, standing right hip to right hip, with the other hand clasped out to the side.

She also showed them the Allemande, Promenade, Roll Away, and Sashay.

Miss Shellman called out, "Circle to your left."

The students held hands and stepped to the beat of the music to their left.

"Circle to your right and go back home."

Some of the boys were still complaining, but they all moved to their right and returned to their starting position.

"Face your partners and Do-si-do."

The students faced their partners, circled one another, and ended facing each other once more.

"Up to the middle and come right back."

Two couples stepped to the center of the square and tapped the hands of the couple standing directly across from them.

"Dancers, swing your partners."

Grayson stood next to Zoey, hip to hip, and placed his arm around her waist. They held hands and walked around in a circle one time.

Don't look at him. Don't look at him, Zoey thought to herself. She could feel him staring at her and she desperately wanted to avoid making eye contact—at least while they were standing so close with his arm around her waist.

Why is he staring at me? Zoey worked up the courage to look up and regretted it immediately.

It was as if his eyes were waiting for hers. He smiled at her while tapping his foot to the beat of the music, and they returned to their home position.

Zoey swore her cheeks were on fire from embarrassment. She looked away so fast that she hoped she didn't get whiplash.

She glanced at Tommi to see if she was just as uncomfortable, but for some reason, Tommi seemed more relaxed. She smiled at Zoey.

Miss Shellman continued to call out steps, and by the third round of calls, everyone seemed to get the hang of the different steps. They all seemed to enjoy themselves—including the boys.

"Great job!" Miss Shellman applauded the effort of her students.

"Looks like we have just enough time for one more dance." She scrolled through her playlist. "I want each group to line up in a single row." She looked over and saw they were now lined up in three rows.

"Spread out a little more. You want to give yourselves plenty of room," she said, then pressed play.

The sound of "Cotton Eye Joe" blared through the gymnasium.

Step tap, step tap. Heel, heel, toe, toe. Grapevine to the side. Zoey spun around with a clap.

"I take it I don't need to teach you this dance." Miss Shellman was surprised most of the students already knew how to do the line dance.

A lot of the students learned it in third grade. Zoey learned it when she used to live in Philly. They had done it whenever someone had a birthday party at the skating rink.

"I hope Mr. Lockwood doesn't come back for the rest of the year," Grayson said and did a lasso spin.

"I thought you said this was corny?" Zoey teased.

"Well, it's not so bad."

Zoey really enjoyed the grapevine and lasso spin.

A few students weren't familiar with the dance, so Miss Shellman worked with them individually.

When Mr. Washburn appeared at the doorway, they knew it was time to go.

"Everyone, grab your things. I'll see you next week." Miss Shellman turned off the music and made sure no one left anything behind.

Chapter 5

Catching Feelings

Mr. Washburn stopped at the restroom after gym class to give his students a quick break. By the time they entered the cafeteria, Emily and Olivia were already seated at their usual table.

"What took you guys so long?" Olivia asked.

"We took a bathroom break after gym." Zoey pulled out a chair and plopped down.

"You'll never guess what Miss Shellman had us do today," Tommi said as she unzipped her lunch bag.

Emily licked some mustard off her finger. "What'd she have you guys do?"

"Square dancing." Tommi opened her bag of carrot sticks.

"Did you say square dancing?" Emily looked confused.

Tommi laughed. "Yep."

"I know it sounds crazy—and I don't even like country music—but it was so much fun!" Zoey sprinkled a few drops of hot sauce on her turkey sandwich.

"Well, I like country music, and it still sounds corny," Olivia said. "I hope she doesn't have us do it."

"Seriously? You guys will totally like it," Zoey took another bite of her sandwich.

Emily and Olivia shared a doubtful look.

"We had to pair up with a boy and get in groups of four couples. Miss Shellman called out the steps and showed us how to do them," Zoey explained.

"Oh, okay. Now I get it," Emily said. "Who'd you pair up with? Josh?"

"No. I was with Grayson." Zoey paused to take a sip of her drink. "Tommi was with Josh."

She leaned in, and her voice was barely above a whisper. "I gotta tell y'all something." Zoey looked around to make sure no one else could hear. "So, at first everything was cool. Grayson and I were having fun, and he was being his silly self. But when Miss Shellman had us 'swing your partner'—"

"That's the part where the boy puts his arm around the girl's waist." Tommi took a bite of her carrot stick.

"Yeah, that part," Zoey said. "When Miss Shellman made that call, all of a sudden something felt weird, and I could feel Grayson staring at me." Zoey leaned back in her seat. "It just felt, I don't know ... kind of strange."

"Hold up! Do you like Grayson?" Olivia asked.

"ABSOLUTELY NOT!"

"Are you sure?" Emily peered at Zoey as if trying to get to the truth. "I mean Grayson is nice, funny, and in case you haven't noticed, he's one of the cutest boys in the entire school."

"Yeah, I'm sure. I mean, I know he's definitely a good guy. But when he was staring at me, it caught me off guard and made me feel funny. And not in a good way."

"Well, boys can be dense. I'm sure he didn't think anything of it," Tommi said. "Each time I looked over at the two of you, it seemed like you were having a good time like everyone else."

"So, you really don't think he noticed anything?"

Tommi held up her finger and finished chewing. "I'm sure of it, Zoey!"

"So, what's the deal with you and Josh? Do you think he could be your secret admirer?" Emily asked before taking the last bite of her hotdog.

"Ugh! Nothing is up with me and Josh. We're just friends. And NO. I don't think he's my secret admirer," Tommi snapped.

"Geesh! You don't need to bite my head off." Emily dabbed at the mustard that had dropped onto her sweater.

"She didn't mean anything, Tommi. Emily was just asking what we are all wondering," Olivia said.

Zoey could sense the tension rising in her friend and could see her nostrils starting to flare. She decided to change the subject.

She patted Tommi on her leg. "I'm looking forward to our field trip tomorrow."

Tommi gently squeezed Zoey's hand and smiled

at her bestie. Zoey knew this meant she was grateful to have the conversation redirected.

"Me too." Emily said. "My mom said it's about a two-hour drive. So, I'm going to bring my headphones and watch a movie on my tablet."

"Okay, cool. I'll make sure I bring my earbuds so I can listen too." Olivia nudged Emily. "We'll have to share, but at least we can both listen."

"Yeah, that's cool. I'll still bring my headphones in case I want to listen to some music." Emily told her.

"Tommi, do you want me to download a movie for us to watch? Or we can just listen to music." Zoey asked.

"Music sounds good to me."

Zoey took the last bite of her sandwich. "Cool! I'll bring some extra snacks too."

"Hey Emily, what time do you want us to come over for the sleepover this weekend?" Tommi asked.

"Six o'clock on Friday," Emily wiped her hands on a napkin. "I wanted to make the time earlier, but my mom said we needed to give people a chance to get home from work."

"Sweet! I'll make sure I get plenty of sleep on Thursday night," Olivia teased.

Zoey laughed. "I know, right!"

The girls finished eating, cleaned up their table, and prepared to head back to class.

"See you tomorrow!" Emily called out as she and Olivia walked over to Mrs. P's line.

Once Zoey and Tommi were alone, Zoey asked. "Are you okay?"

Tommi looked a little confused. "Yeah. Why'd you ask?"

"Because you seemed upset when Emily asked about you and Josh."

Tommi's tone became harsh. "I'm tired of people asking me about him. I mean, I already said there's nothing going on, and I don't think he's my secret admirer!"

Zoey placed a hand on her friend's shoulder to calm her. "Okay. Okay. I'll admit I thought something was up, but if you say it's not, then I won't bring it up again. And I'll beat up anyone who does." Zoey smiled, hoping to lighten the mood.

Tommi laughed. "We need to go before Mr.

Washburn gives us both detention for holding up the class."

They joined their classmates in line.

"So glad you two decided to join us," Mr. Washburn teased.

As they walked back to class, Zoey thought it looked like Tommi wanted to say something.

"Everything good?" Zoey asked.

Tommi nodded her head yes.

Zoey felt like something was up but decided not to press.

When they reached their lockers, she unlocked the combination on hers and put away her lunch tote. Before she closed the door, she saw a note stuck in the vent. Zoey looked around instinctively to see who it was from. She unfolded the lined paper and froze.

> *Hey Zoey,*
> *I think you're cute, and I really like you.*
> *Do you like me?*
> *Grayson*
> *PS: You don't have to write me back; you can just tell me.*

She quickly spun around to see if anyone saw her read the note. Her heart was racing. *Oh my God! What am I gonna do?* She wasn't ready to face Grayson yet. *Maybe I can act like I didn't get the note.* She went over it once more to make sure she didn't misread it.

"Ugh! Why does he have to like me?" she grumbled under her breath. She slammed her locker door and headed to class.

Fortunately, a few other students were entering the room at the same time as Zoey. Her eyes tried to avoid looking Grayson's way, but because he sat directly behind her, it was practically impossible.

"Take out your math homework so we can review the problems." Mr. Washburn pushed up the sleeves to his fitted coffee-colored sweater.

Zoey reached to retrieve her folder from her backpack, and when she turned around, she found Grayson's eyes waiting for hers once again. He smiled, and Zoey turned around so fast, she dang near hurt her neck.

That afternoon was a blur. Mr. Washburn went over all ten math problems. They reviewed a combination of decimal and fraction related word problems. Zoey ignored Grayson the entire afternoon and couldn't wait for school to be over. They covered a reading and comprehension lesson and a social studies lesson. Mr. Washburn said he wanted everything to be fresh in their minds since they were visiting the State Capital the next day.

Once the bell rang, Zoey flew out of the room and rushed to get her belongings from her locker. Luckily, she started packing her things and cleaned off her desk a few minutes early to ensure a quick getaway.

Just as she closed her locker, she turned around.

"Hey! Did you get my note?" Grayson asked.

Oh shoot! If only he had waited a couple more seconds, she would have been out of there.

"Sorry, Grayson, I gotta go! My mom is waiting for me." Zoey rushed past him in a hurry. "Talk to you tomorrow." She didn't dare look back.

When Zoey got home, she hung up her coat, placed her lunch bag on the counter, dropped her backpack at the bottom of her bed, and went to find Jasmine for some sisterly advice.

"Jazz! Where are you?" she called throughout the house.

"What's up?" Jasmine poked her head outside the doorway of her bedroom.

"You're not going to believe what happened today!" Zoey blurted and dragged herself to her sister's room.

Jasmine chuckled. "Aw c'mon, whatever it is, it couldn't be that bad."

Zoey fell onto Jasmine's bed and let out a loud sigh. "Oh, yes, it is."

"So, what happened?"

"Ugh! Grayson went and ruined everything!"

Jasmine looked confused. "Grayson?"

Zoey rolled her eyes and sat up on the edge of the bed. "Here, read this." She handed the folded note to her sister.

Jasmine read the note out loud.

> "Hey Zoey,
> I think you're cute, and I really like you.
> Do you like me?
> Grayson
> PS: You don't have to write me back; you can just tell me."

She handed the note to Zoey. "Aw! So, he likes you. What's wrong with that?"

"Everything!" Zoey threw up her arms. "He had to go and ruin a perfectly good friendship, that's what's wrong!"

"The friendship isn't ruined, Zo. You and Grayson can still be friends. Things will only be awkward if you make them that way." Jasmine frowned. "Oh my God! I sound just like mom."

Zoey chuckled. "Yeah, you kind of do."

"So, what did you say after he gave you the note?"

Zoey's eyes looked like they were going to pop out of her head. "Nothing! I ignored him all afternoon."

"Zoey!" Jasmine snapped. "You've gotta give the boy an answer." She softened her voice and asked, "Do you like him?"

"Sure. I mean, we're friends. And I like him way better than Jackson. I never really thought about him like a boyfriend." Zoey thought for a moment. "Plus, I don't even think I want a boyfriend."

"The note didn't ask you to be his girlfriend. He said he thought you were cute and wanted to know if you liked him." Jasmine pulled her binder out of her backpack. "Don't make it awkward, Zo. You said you guys are already friends, and you like him. So, I think you can tell him yes, you like him."

Zoey's voice was frantic. "But what if he thinks I want to be his girlfriend?"

Jasmine took a few short steps and sat next to Zoey on the bed. "It's okay to let him know you got his note and that yes you like him. You can even write him a note. You don't have to verbally respond. And if he comes back with another note or asks you directly to be his girlfriend, then you can tell him you only want to be friends." Jasmine placed her hand on top of Zoey's hand. "Does that work for you?"

Zoey smiled and nodded. "Yes."

"Remember, sis, nothing has to change. Simply act like you do every day. Things don't have to get weird."

"Tomorrow, we have our field trip, so I'll get there early and put a note in his locker." Zoey felt much better and stood to leave. "Thanks, Jazz."

Jasmine gave her sister a hug. "See what happens

when you go all Zoey 2.0 on 'em!" Jasmine teased. "He wasn't ready for the glow up."

"I guess not." Zoey laughed.

"Okay, now get out of here. I gotta do my homework."

Feeling a bit better after talking to Jasmine and coming up with a plan on how to proceed with Grayson, Zoey headed to the kitchen for a quick snack.

She arranged five pizza bagels on a plate and returned the bag to the freezer. She put the dish in the microwave for seventy-five seconds. She poured a glass of cranberry juice and grabbed a napkin from the drawer. When the microwave dinged, she removed the plate and sprinkled a few splashes of hot sauce on the bagel bites.

She replayed the events of the day as she sat at the kitchen table. *When I finish eating, I need to send a group text to the girls and tell them what happened. I knew I wasn't imagining things earlier in gym class. I could tell something was weird, and now, I know why.* Initially, Zoey thought she may have misread the situation when they were learning how to square dance. But now, she knew her intuition was correct.

Whenever someone has something important or some juicy tea, the girls share it in the group text. Zoey finished her snack and put her dishes in the dishwasher, then went to her room to figure out what she wanted to say in her note to Grayson.

First things first, Zoey thought to herself. She grabbed her phone from her backpack and laid across her bed and sent a group text.

> **ZOEY:** "ur not going to believe what happened today!"

Zoey didn't actually have any homework, but she decided to review her spelling words for the test on Friday. She was on the second word, *ancestor.* "A-n-c-e-s-t-o-r," she spelled it out loud, and then checked to see if she was correct.

She heard her phone ding and picked it up. As she checked her messages, two more notifications came through.

> **OLIVIA:** "what's up Zoey"

TOMMI: "what happened???"

EMILY: "👀 tea?"

ZOEY: "when I went to my locker after lunch, I found a note from Grayson"

TOMMI: "wait . . . what?"

OLIVIA: "what'd it say?"

ZOEY: "He said he thought I was cute and told me he liked me." Zoey's fingers were striking the phone keys lightning fast.

TOMMI: "OMG!!! he finally told you😊"

ZOEY: "what'd u mean . . . he finally told me???"

TOMMI: "I knew he liked u but he told me not to say anything

ZOEY: "ugh"

EMILY: "this is juicy"

EMILY: "what'd u say?"

OLIVIA: "sounds like he wants u to be his gf"

ZOEY: "he wants to know if I like him"

OLIVIA: "do u???"

ZOEY: "I like him but not enough to be his gf"

TOMMI: "what're u gonna do?"

ZOEY: "I'm gonna write him a note back . . . still trying to figure out what to say, BUT I'm not gonna be his gf."

> **EMILY:** "let's talk about this tomorrow on the bus"
>
> **OLIVIA:** "sounds good to me"
>
> **TOMMI:** "call me if you need to talk"
>
> **ZOEY:** "K byee"

Zoey put away her phone. *Ugh! Why'd he have to go and mess everything up?* She picked up her tablet and started reviewing the remainder of her spelling words. *Communicate.* She spelled it out loud and checked to see if it was correct. Once she'd finished going over the spelling list, she pulled a piece of loose-leaf paper from her three-ring binder.

She bit the inside of her cheek and tried to figure out what she wanted to say.

> *Grayson,*
> *I'm glad you think I'm cute. I do like you ... as a friend.*
> *Zoey* ☺

She read over the letter once more and was pleased with what she wrote. She folded the note and put it in her backpack for safe keeping. She'd make sure she got to school early tomorrow and put it in his locker before he got there. He rode the bus, so she usually arrived at school before most of the bus riders.

Later that evening, the Lyndon family sat down to a dinner of savory pot roast and seasoned vegetables, cornbread, and gravy.

"Mom, don't forget Emily is having a sleepover this Friday." Zoey dipped a piece of cornbread in the tasty brown gravy.

"I didn't forget. Her mother texted me and told me to drop you off at six o'clock."

"Not that I don't appreciate this good meal, but isn't Tuesdays usually taco night?" Zoey's dad asked his wife.

"I know! But I felt like having a pot roast," she said as she wiped her mouth with her napkin.

"Well, I for one don't mind the switch up, Mom,"

Jasmine said. "It's like having Sunday dinner in the middle of the week."

"I'm with you on that." He winked at Jasmine. "If I wasn't already married to your mama, I'd ask her to marry me just for her cooking." Mr. Lyndon teased and smiled at their mother.

She flicked her hand and smiled back. "David, you are such a flirt."

"I'm serious," he laughed. "Girls, y'all better take notes from your mama if y'all wanna be able to throw down in the kitchen."

"Daddy, Mommy is already teaching me to cook. She lets me help with the baked mac and lasagna when she makes it," Jasmine boasted.

Zoey didn't know if she would ever be as good of a cook as her mother and wasn't in a hurry to learn. For now, she was content with making pizza bagels in the microwave or making a grilled cheese sandwich.

"Mom, can you take me to school a little early tomorrow?" Zoey asked.

Her mother stuck her fork into a small piece of beef. "Why do you need to get to school early tomorrow?"

"Remember, we have a field trip to Jeff City."

"Oh, that's right. I wasn't able to be a chaperone this time," her mom replied.

"Also, I need to get to school early because I want to talk to Mr. Washburn about a test we have coming up." Zoey neglected to share the real reason she wanted to get to school early. Her mom didn't need to know about the note to Grayson.

"Daddy, can you drop me and Aubrey off at the movies on Saturday?" Jasmine asked.

"Sure, just let me know what time."

"Is Case gonna be there?" Zoey teased and immediately regretted it after feeling a kick to her chin under the table.

Jasmine gave her sister the stink eye. "Yeah. We're meeting up with a few of our friends from school, if you must know."

"That sounds like fun," Mrs. Lyndon said.

Zoey looked between her parents. "What are you two gonna do when Jasmine and I are both busy doing stuff with our friends or when we go to college?"

"They'll probably be bored out of their minds," Jasmine teased.

"I'm sure we'll find some way to keep ourselves entertained." Her dad gave their mom an exaggerated wink.

Mrs. Lyndon shook her head and tried to hide a smile.

"Really, Dad?" Jasmine looked disgusted. "We're trying to eat."

Mr. Lyndon laughed in spite of himself and ate a forkful of gravy-covered beef.

"We got to make our own video game today using coding in class," Zoey told them.

"Wow! That's great they're teaching you about coding," her dad said. "Coding is a wonderful skill because so much of what we use at work uses program codes."

"It seemed a little tricky at first, but after a while I got the hang of it, and it was fun."

"We use industrial robots in some of our plants to do welding," Mr. Lyndon shared.

"Wow! That's so cool!" Zoey was impressed.

"Yeah, it really is. Whenever I have to visit one of the plants, I'm always amazed," her dad agreed.

Once the family finished eating dinner, Zoey and Jasmine started clearing the table. Their mom put the leftovers in storage containers and the girls finished cleaning the kitchen.

Afterward, the girls both practiced playing their instruments before getting their clothes ready for the next day, then finally preparing for bed.

Chapter 6

Things Get Messy

The next morning, Zoey got ready earlier than usual. She set her alarm to give her twenty extra minutes. She made her bed, fluffed her pillows, and tucked her pajamas behind them. Since she wrapped her hair the night before and set out her school clothes, it didn't take her long to get ready. She wore a pair of light gray corduroys, a yellow and gray sweater, and a dark gray infinity scarf. She looked herself over in the full-length mirror that hung on the back of her closet door and combed through her hair once more. Pleased with how she looked, she put on her gold hoop earrings.

She double checked her backpack and saw the note she'd written to Grayson safely tucked away. She made sure she had her sugar poppy lip gloss, zipped her bag, and headed downstairs for breakfast.

"Morning, Zo!" Jasmine was already seated at the table eating a piece of bacon.

Zoey dropped her backpack in the corner of the kitchen and took a bowl from the cabinet. "Good morning, Jazz!"

"There's still some bacon left." Jasmine pointed to a covered plate on the counter.

"I'm just gonna have some cereal. I'm not that hungry." Zoey pulled the box of cereal from the pantry and removed the carton of milk from the refrigerator, then poured it into her bowl. She snagged a piece of bacon after returning the milk to the fridge and the cereal to the shelf.

"Thought you didn't want any bacon," Jasmine said as she finished off her orange juice.

"I didn't—until I smelled it." Zoey took a bite of the maple flavored bacon.

"Did you write your boy a note?" Jasmine asked.

Zoey rolled her eyes. "He's not my boy. And yes,

I wrote him a note." Zoey scooped up a spoonful of cereal. "I'm gonna slip it into his locker like we talked about, and hopefully that will be the end of it."

"Welp, I'm sure everything will be fine. But just remember to stay cool. Don't make things awkward by acting weird." Jasmine finished her breakfast and put her dishes in the dishwasher.

"Ugh! I'm not going to do anything stupid. I'll just act like I always do."

"Uh-huh. Okay, if you say so." Jasmine sounded doubtful.

Zoey continued eating her breakfast.

Mrs. Lyndon entered the kitchen and put the tea kettle on. "Good morning, girls."

"Morning, Mom!" the girls replied.

"Zoey, what time do you want to leave?" her mom asked.

"How about ten to eight?" Zoey suggested. "That should give me more than enough time to talk to Mr. Washburn."

Mrs. Lyndon placed a tea bag into her cup and waited for the kettle to boil. "Jasmine, don't forget your sheet music. I saw you left it on the music stand."

"Oh, shoot! Thanks Mom. I'm definitely gonna need it today." Jasmine ran to grab it.

Mrs. Lyndon poured some steaming water into her cup and sat at the table, while Zoey finished eating her breakfast.

"Jasmine!" The girl's mom yelled. "You need to get—"

"I know! I know! I'm leaving now." Jasmine grabbed her coat from the hallway closet, put it on, and threw her backpack over her shoulder. "See ya later!" She called out as she left for the bus stop.

"Bye, Jazz." Their mom and Zoey replied.

Zoey rinsed out her bowl and spoon, then placed them in the dishwasher. Since she was ready for school, she returned to the table and chatted with her mom while she finished her tea.

Usually when Zoey got dropped off at school, there were a ton of cars in the car rider line. But this morning when Mrs. Lyndon pulled up in front of the school, there wasn't anyone in line.

"See ya, Mom!" Zoey said as she jumped out of their jeep and slammed the door behind her.

Once inside the building, Zoey walked down the

empty halls. The only people there were the teachers drinking their coffee and preparing for the students to arrive. When Zoey got to the fifth-grade hallway, she made a beeline to her locker and put away her coat and lunch. She sat her backpack on the floor and pulled out the note she wrote for Grayson. She looked around to make sure no one else was there, then slid the folded paper into the vent of his locker. She checked once more to make sure she hadn't been seen, then let out a sigh of relief.

Now let me go and talk to Mr. Washburn.

Zoey entered her classroom and greeted her teacher. "Good morning!"

"Hey, Zoey!" Mr. Washburn looked a bit surprised. "What are you doing here so early?"

"My mom had an appointment and needed to drop me off earlier than usual." *Lord, please forgive me for telling a lie. But I can't very well tell him I was having a crisis and needed to get here early to slip a note into Grayson's locker.*

"Oh, I understand," he said and continued tapping the keys on his laptop.

"What time are we leaving this morning?" Zoey asked.

"We'll start loading the buses at eight forty-five."

Zoey pulled her cell phone and earbuds out of her backpack and played a game of Candy Crush while she waited for her classmates to arrive. She was on her fourth level when Josh and some of the other car-rider kids started to arrive.

"Wassup, Zoey?" Josh gave her a nod and took his seat.

Zoey removed her ear buds and placed them in her desk. "Hey, Josh. Just looking forward to this field trip."

"I know. Field trips are almost as good as getting a snow day." He leaned toward her and placed his elbows on his desk.

Getting a whiff of something, Zoey leaned in and sniffed. "Are you wearing cologne?"

Josh leaned his head back and laughed. "Dang, girl! Why are you tripping?"

"I'm sorry. I didn't mean to be rude. It's just, you've never worn cologne before."

"I'm not wearing cologne. It's just Axe." He smiled.

Zoey noticed some of the bus riders had arrived, and Grayson entered the room. *Just be cool and don't stare at him,* she thought to herself. Zoey casually looked in his direction but continued her conversation with Josh.

Grayson greeted Josh with the usual bro-man head nod. "Wassup?" Then he shifted his gaze to Zoey. "Hey, Zoey, what y'all over here talking about?"

"I was trying to find out why Josh is suddenly wearing cologne," she answered.

Grayson chuckled. "Bruh! Who're you wearing cologne for?"

"Aw, man. Shut up!" Josh shot Grayson an icy look.

"Wait! What?" Zoey's curiosity had been piqued. "Josh, who're you wearing cologne for?"

Josh was clearly irritated with his friends. "Y'all really need to stop sweating me! Zoey, I already told you I'm not wearing cologne."

Grayson seemed to enjoy his friend's discomfort. "Whatever, bruh!" He sighed and asked Josh about a basketball game that was on last night.

Zoey thought about Grayson's comment and wondered if Josh was wearing Axe because he liked a girl. *Why wouldn't he tell me? We talk about everything.* Zoey knew Axe was a body spray that some boys liked to wear. She also wanted to figure out what was going on with Josh. She noticed he'd been a little distant lately. She was grateful Grayson was content talking to Josh and that he didn't ask her about their notes.

After all the students arrived, Mr. Washburn took care of attendance, morning announcements, and reminded his class to be on their best behavior. He let the students know what he considered acceptable behavior before getting on the bus.

"I'll not tolerate disrespectful students on this trip. You'll respect every teacher, chaperone, and your fellow students both on and off the bus. If I see anyone not following the rules you've all previously agreed to when you turned in your permission slips, you'll get detention." Mr. Washburn scanned the room. "Do I make myself clear?"

The students all answered yes.

When it was time to load the bus, Mr. Washburn's class made a pit stop at the restrooms before heading outside to the buses.

After using the restroom, Zoey remembered she put her earbuds in her desk. She approached her teacher. "Mr. Washburn, I left my earbuds in my desk. Can I run and get them?"

He looked at his watch. "Yes. Hurry up, we'll be getting on the bus soon."

"I will!" She turned to Tommi. "Save me a seat!"

She ran all the way to her room and quickly retrieved her earbuds. Her class was in line behind Mrs. P's, and hopefully they hadn't gotten on the bus yet. She ran all the way back and was out of breath when she caught up to her class. Mr. Washburn was there, waiting for her.

"Go ahead and find a seat." He told her as he checked her name off his clipboard.

Zoey stepped onto the bus and looked to see where Tommi was sitting. *You've gotta be kidding me! Why is Josh sitting with Tommi?* She saw that Tommi hadn't saved her a seat, and because some of Mrs. P's students were on the bus too, there were barely any spots left.

When Zoey got to Tommi, she asked, "Why didn't you save me a seat?"

"I'm sorry, Zo! Mr. Washburn told us not to hold seats."

"He knew I was coming right back, you could've—"

"Trouble in paradise?" Trudy interrupted from the seat behind Tommi and Josh.

"Oh, shut up, Trudy! Nobody is even talking to you." Zoey rolled her eyes.

"You can sit with me," Grayson stood and waved her over to his seat.

Zoey looked around, but the only two seats available were with Trudy or Grayson. *This is just great!*

"Zoey, you need to sit down so we can go," Mr. Washburn instructed.

She decided to sit next to Grayson because she knew Trudy would get on her nerves after sitting with her for two hours.

Grayson stepped into the aisle to allow Zoey to sit by the window. "I like to sit on the end," he said.

"That's fine." She knew because of his height that he would be more comfortable closest to the aisle. "Thanks," she said with a half-smile.

She was mad at Tommi for not saving her a seat and wondered why in the heck Josh and Grayson didn't sit together, anyway! She stared out the window as the bus pulled off. Zoey took a couple of deep breaths to get her emotions in check. When she looked over at Grayson, she found his eyes waiting for hers.

There was an awkward silence. She knew he wanted to talk about the notes, but thankfully he didn't bring up the subject.

"Are you looking forward to seeing the State Capital?" he asked.

"Yeah, I am."

"Me too. I wish we'd have more field trips. There's lots of educational stuff we can do outside of school."

Zoey agreed.

Grayson pulled a pack of bubble gum from his backpack. "Would you like a piece?"

"Yes, please."

They both chewed the sugary sweetness, and Zoey pulled her earbuds and cell phone from her backpack.

"So, you got my note?" he asked.

Oh no! Don't panic, just be cool.

"Yeah, I got it." She glanced at him. "Did you see the one I left for you this morning?"

He smiled. "Yeah. I did."

Zoey was nervous and softened her voice. She didn't want anyone to overhear their conversation. "So, you think I'm cute?" She smiled and selected her words carefully. "I'm not really sure what to make of that."

Grayson lowered his tone. "I just wanted you to know that I like you. I mean, I think you're really cool, and I would like to get to know you better."

Zoey could tell he was nervous by the way he kept rubbing his hands together. She was glad it wasn't just her. *Grayson's always been a likable guy, but he is always such a goof.* However, now, she was seeing him in a different light. *He seems more serious and genuine.* Zoey shook off her thoughts and focused on what he was saying.

Not knowing how to respond, she didn't say anything.

"Would you like to come to one of my basketball games?" he asked.

Oh Lord! Did this boy just ask me on a date?

Zoey's heart started racing a mile a minute.

"And don't worry! This is not a date," he said calmly. "A lot of people come out to our games, especially on Saturday mornings. In fact, your girl Olivia comes a lot because her cousin plays on the team."

Feeling better and her heart rate returning to normal, she answered, "I didn't know you played basketball. I thought you were into football?"

He chuckled. "I play both. Football is definitely my favorite sport, but I also enjoy playing basketball." He paused for a moment. "So do you think you'd like to come and check out my game this Saturday?"

Not seeing any way out of this situation, she answered, "Sure! I'll see if I can come with Olivia."

"Cool!" Grayson's face lit up like he just hit the jackpot.

What have I gotten myself into? Ugh! Why didn't Tommi just save me a stupid seat?

Grayson told Zoey he had two older brothers who both played basketball, so naturally, he played too. His brothers only played basketball, and he was the only one who played both sports.

She didn't know he had older brothers, and she enjoyed listening to him talk about his family. *Maybe going to one of his games won't be so bad.*

They talked the entire trip, and Zoey realized Grayson was easy to talk to. She told him she liked to make jewelry, and they discovered they both took piano lessons and hated mayonnaise.

"You're real chill!" Grayson said. "I was hoping I didn't freak you out with my note."

"Why would you think that?" Zoey asked.

"Because when I tried to talk to you after school yesterday, you ran out of the building so fast that I thought you might hurt yourself trying to get away from me."

Zoey couldn't hold back her laugh. "Sorry about that."

"I realized you probably thought I was asking you to be my girlfriend." He stretched his leg into the aisle.

"So, you weren't asking me to be your girlfriend?" Zoey asked.

"No! Not at all. But I could tell that's what you thought," Grayson said and rubbed his knee.

Geesh! What a relief! "Honestly, I wasn't sure," Zoey admitted.

"I just wanted you to know I like you and would like to get to know you better."

Filled with relief, Zoey smiled. "I think I'd like that."

"Cool."

Zoey could tell he was trying to hold back a smile, and that made her warm inside.

Later, when they arrived at the State Capital Zoey was surprised by how large the building was. The group was scheduled for a thirty-minute guided tour. The building was simply breathtaking, and apparently, it had recently undergone a massive renovation.

The students got to see the House of Representatives and where the Speaker of the House sits when they're in session. Zoey was amazed by the beautiful stained-glass windows, and she thought the Legislative Lounge looked more like a fancy library with its dark wood and tons of books. The Senate was directly located across the hall from the House of Representatives. The pinkish-colored ceilings and gigantic columns in The Senate were quite impressive. The tour guide was knowledgeable about the history of Missouri and shared interesting facts about it throughout the tour. The state seal was placed throughout the building. The students learned it was designed by Robert Wells in 1822, and the state of Missouri is just over 200 years old.

Once the tour was over, the class headed to the museum to check out some of the exhibits. Mr. Washburn allowed them to break into smaller groups and assigned a chaperone to each one.

Since Emily's mother, Mrs. Elle, was one of the chaperones, Mr. Washburn allowed Zoey and Tommi to go with her group.

"Hey, Mrs. Elle!" Zoey waved and greeted Emily's mom as she joined them.

"Hello, girls!" she said with outstretched arms. She gave Zoey and Tommi a motherly hug.

Emily ran up to Zoey and locked arms with her.

"So, how did it go this morning? I saw you sitting with Grayson."

"Shh! You don't have to be so loud," Zoey said, looking around to make sure no one was listening.

"Sorry! What happened?" Emily whispered.

"Everything's fine. I wasn't expecting to sit with him. I was supposed to sit with Tommi." Zoey turned her attention to her bestie. "Why didn't you save me a seat? You knew I had to run back to class for my earbuds."

"I told you; Mr. Washburn wasn't letting us save seats," Tommi answered and looked away.

"But why didn't you tell Josh I was sitting there? He would have sat with Grayson."

"I don't know, Zoey! I didn't think about holding the seat once Mr. Washburn told us we couldn't, plus I didn't think it was such a big deal," Tommi replied.

Zoey stared at Tommi and tried to figure out why she was acting like such a smart aleck. *I'm starting to think Tommi and Josh like each other. But I asked her about it, and she denied it. Plus, wouldn't Josh tell me if he liked Tommi?*

"Whatever, Tommi." Zoey directed her attention to Olivia and Emily. "Basically, he let me know he likes me and wants to get to know me." Zoey tried hiding her smile.

"Does he want you to be his girlfriend?" Olivia asked.

"Yeah, what does that even mean?" Emily wanted to know.

"He said he wasn't asking me to be his girlfriend. He just likes me. And he wants me to come watch him play basketball." Zoey let her smile show.

"Oh! Sounds like Zoey's getting a boyfriend!" Emily teased and bumped Zoey with her hip.

The girls giggled and continued exploring the exhibits. They were discussing the exhibit on Frontier Living when Trudy came running up to them, dragging some boy behind her.

"Look who I ran into!" Trudy gushed.

"Oh my God! Zoey, it's Bradley!" Tommi said, surprised.

Bradley Thompson was a boy Zoey, Tommi, and Trudy met at summer camp. And he happened to have a crush on Tommi.

"Hey, Zoey." Bradley smiled and gave her a

quick wave. "It's good to see you guys." He gave Tommi a hug.

Emily and Olivia were both grinning because they had already heard about Tommi's summer crush. They also saw a couple of pictures Zoey and Tommi took before they left camp.

Trudy felt the need to make the introductions. "This is Bradley from the green team. We all met him this past summer at camp."

Last summer, all of the campers were identified by the color of T-shirt they wore. Zoey, Tommi, and Trudy were on the lavender team.

Bradley chuckled. "It's actually Bradley Thompson." He flashed a smile in Olivia and Emily's direction. "Nice to meet you both."

Zoey noticed Grayson, Josh, and Jackson watching them from a short distance away.

"It's crazy running into all of you." Bradley shook his head in disbelief. "Trudy, I'm glad I found you, otherwise I wouldn't have had the chance to see Tommi and Zoey. My school got here when the building first opened so now, we're getting ready to leave. I'm glad I got the chance to catch up with you." He turned to Tommi. "Tommi, did you get a chance to check out *Ant-Man and the Wasp*?"

"Oh, yeah. I remember you two were really into the Marvel movies." Zoey ignored Grayson and Josh, who were still watching them.

"I'm hoping to check it out this weekend," he replied. "Hey, I see my group over there. I need to go, but it was great seeing all of you again." He gave them a parting wave and rejoined his class, who were getting ready to leave the gift shop.

"Tommi, I know you showed us a picture of you and Bradley when you came home from camp last summer, but he is way cuter in person," Olivia teased.

"He's definitely cuter than I remembered," Zoey said before checking her phone for the time.

Mrs. Elle asked, "Trudy, which group are you with?"

Trudy pointed to her group. "I'm with Mr. Washburn. Right over there."

"It looks like he's waiting on you, dear," Mrs. Elle replied.

"Thanks, Trudy, for bringing Bradley over," Tommi said.

"No problem." Trudy left to join her group.

Zoey and her friends explored quite a few more exhibits in the museum before finally ending up at the gift shop, then heading for lunch. Each of the girls looked to see what items they wanted to purchase. Zoey got a commemorative Missouri penny and a T-shirt. Tommi got a T-shirt and a Cardinals pencil. Emily and Olivia purchased sweatshirts. Once everyone completed their purchases, Mrs. Elle told them it was time to meet up with their class in the cafeteria.

"Mrs. Elle, do you mind if we stop at the restroom?" Zoey asked.

"Sure." She looked at the other girls and asked, "Does anyone else need to use the bathroom?"

The girls all answered no. Since Mr. Washburn and their classmates were already standing outside the cafeteria, Mrs. Elle walked the girls over and left them with their class. She told Mr. Washburn she was taking Zoey to the restroom. Emily decided at the last minute she would go too.

After walking the short distance down the corridor, the girls used the facilities, washed their hands, and returned to the café to join their class. Once inside the cafeteria, Mrs. Elle could see Tommi and Olivia seated at a round table and instructed the girls to join their friends. She told them she would sit with the other chaperones at a table nearby.

"I'll meet you at the table. I want to see if they have a straw," Zoey told Emily.

"I can walk with you."

Jackson, Grayson, and Josh were seated at the table next to the section with the condiments, napkins, and utensils. When Zoey approached, she overheard Grayson teasing Josh about having to keep his girlfriend a secret.

Zoey wasn't trying to be nosy, so she found the straws, grabbed one, and turned to head to the table with her friends. Suddenly, something Josh said made her freeze in her tracks. She and Emily stared at one another because they both overheard the same thing.

"Did he just say—"

"Tommi!" Emily finished Zoey's sentence.

Emily and Zoey stared at one another in disbelief with their mouths open. The girls rushed to join their friends for lunch, but then Zoey stopped midstep. She turned around and went to confront Josh.

"Did you just say Tommi's your girlfriend?" she blurted.

Josh and Grayson turned to look at Zoey.

"What?" Josh stammered.

Zoey could tell from their facial expressions that she'd caught them off guard.

"Emily and I were getting a straw when we overheard you say Tommi's your girlfriend."

Josh shook his head and let out a huge sigh. "Yeah, we've been dating."

"So why keep it a secret? Especially from your friends!" Emily asked, clearly confused.

"Look, it wasn't my idea to keep us a secret." Josh crossed his arms.

"Are you saying that was Tommi's idea?" Zoey asked.

"What I'm saying is, you need to talk to your friend." Josh turned his focus to Grayson and Jackson.

Zoey and Emily left to join Tommi and Olivia. Zoey's thoughts were racing. *Why would Tommi keep their relationship a secret? I asked her point-blank if she liked Josh. Why would she lie?*

"None of this makes any sense," Zoey mumbled.

"I know!" Emily agreed. "I was just thinking the same thing."

When they reached the lunch table, Tommi was eating a sandwich and Olivia munched on a salad.

"There you are. We thought you fell in," Olivia teased.

Zoey placed her lunch bag on the table. "Tommi! How long have you and Josh been dating?"

Tommi froze.

"Tommi and Josh aren't dating!" Olivia chuckled and took another bite of her salad.

"Yes, they are. Josh just told us," Emily said.

"I asked you a question." Zoey waited for Tommi to answer.

With her head dropped, Tommi placed her sandwich on the napkin in front of her. "We started dating after Christmas break."

"Tommi! That was six weeks ago!" Zoey was shocked.

"Wait a minute! You and Josh have been dating for six weeks, and you never told us?" Olivia asked in disbelief.

"No. It's only been five weeks." Tommi lowered

her voice and glanced around to see if anyone was looking at them.

"Really, Tommi!" Zoey placed a hand on her hip. "I know for a fact I asked you if you liked Josh or if you thought he liked you. And you flat out denied it." Zoey paused and chose her words carefully. "I thought we were friends!"

"It's not like I have to tell you everything," Tommi snapped.

Zoey grabbed her lunch bag off the table and was clearly upset. "I know you don't have to tell me everything Tommi, but you also don't have to lie to my face," Zoey huffed. "That was shady!" Zoey's feelings were hurt, and she no longer wanted to sit with Tommi for lunch. She saw a few other empty tables nearby and chose to sit alone so that she could cool off.

"Not cool, Tommi. Not cool." Emily scolded her friend, then picked up her lunch and joined Zoey at the other table.

A few moments later, Olivia joined Zoey and Emily.

"You guys didn't have to follow me." Zoey was

surprised Emily and Olivia didn't stay with Tommi. "I'm so mad. I just had to step away."

Emily agreed. "I get it. My feelings are hurt too because I thought we shared everything, and it seems like Tommi went out of her way to keep this a secret from us."

"How in the heck did we miss this?" Olivia asked.

That's simple. She didn't want us to know. And she lied about it so we wouldn't find out. Zoey decided to keep her thoughts to herself.

The girls finished their lunch and prepared to return to school. When they loaded the bus, Zoey sat with Olivia since Emily rode home with her mother. Tommi and Josh sat together, and Grayson had a seat to himself. Zoey and Olivia talked about attending the basketball game on Saturday. Both girls decided to listen to music for the remainder of the trip.

Chapter 7
Jasmine's Time To Shine

When Zoey got home from school, her mom reminded her they would be attending Jasmine's winter concert. Because of all the drama with Tommi, Zoey had completely forgotten about it. She knew her sister had been practicing a lot and was happy she was asked to play first chair. Jasmine was still at school because of the event.

Zoey decided to talk to her mother about the fallout between her and Tommi. She told her about her suspicions over the past few weeks and how she felt something was off with Tommi and Josh, but Tommi consistently denied anything was going on. Her mother listened patiently and encouraged Zoey to share her feelings.

"Sweety, I'm sorry you and Tommi had a fight." Mrs. Lyndon walked over to the armchair where Zoey was sitting, then gave her a hug and sat on the ottoman next to it. "I understand why your feelings are hurt, but I'm sure you two will be able to work through this."

"I know she doesn't have to tell me everything. But I came right out and asked her a couple of times, and basically, she chose to tell a bold face lie to my face," Zoey said as she picked at her fingernails.

"I think the reason she wasn't honest with you is the same reason she wanted to keep her relationship a secret."

"What's that?" Zoey asked.

"A relationship is a commitment between two people and not something you should be ashamed of. I think Tommi isn't ready to have a boyfriend. Being in a relationship takes work. Honestly, none of you girls should even be thinking about dating at your age."

"Emily's having a sleepover this weekend. With

everyone mad at her, Tommi might not even show up." Zoey sighed.

"Oh, I wouldn't worry about that." Her mom gave her a little grin. "I'm sure Tonya will make sure she's there."

"Do you think Ms. Tonya will make her come to the sleepover?"

"I sure do. Especially after learning her daughter has fallen out with her friends," she said reassuringly. "Now, go on upstairs and freshen up before we have to leave. I want to get to Jasmin's school early."

"Okay, Mom." Zoey gave her mother a big hug and went upstairs to change her outfit.

Zoey's parents were real sticklers about being on time, so they made a habit of arriving early for school events. Zoey remembered how her mom got upset last year with the parents trying to save entire rows of seats for friends and family members. When they entered the auditorium, they were able to find three seats in the front row.

"Jasmine should be coming out soon," Mrs. Lyndon said, thumbing through the program.

"Daddy, you forgot to bring in her flowers," Zoey whispered.

"I'm going to run out at the end of the program and get them. I don't want to hold them throughout the concert."

A short while later, the auditorium started to fill up. The members of the orchestra came out and began tuning their instruments. Jasmine looked over and saw her family seated in the front row and gave them a short wave.

Their father pulled out his camera, then selected which lens he would use to capture the best pictures. Once he positioned the proper lens, he snapped a few quick shots. The school dimmed the lights in the auditorium, and everyone found their seats. After a few brief announcements from the principal, the concert began.

The first selection was the theme song from *Pirates of the Caribbean.*

"They sound good!" Mrs. Lyndon whispered.

Dad was listening intently and agreed.

Zoey couldn't believe how intense the music

was, yet somehow relaxing at the same time. The second piece they played was a classical number called "Danse Macabre" and it was much softer. Zoey actually nodded off because it was so relaxing. The orchestra played several more selections, but the last song of the evening was "Bohemian Rhapsody" and it seemed to be a crowd favorite.

Jasmine played with poise and grace; her entire family was so proud of how well she did. Mr. Lyndon slipped out at the beginning of "Bohemian Rhapsody" and made it back to his seat just as the orchestra was finishing the finale.

Jasmine made her way through the crowd and caught up to where her parents and Zoey were waiting.

"Congratulations!" Her father greeted her with a beautiful bouquet of hydrangeas, lilies, pink and white roses, and daisies.

"Thanks, Daddy!" Jasmine took the flowers and couldn't resist bringing them to her nose because they were so fragrant.

Her mom gave her a big hug. "You played beautifully."

"All those lessons are paying off," her father teased.

"Good job, Jazz!" It was Zoey's turn to hug her sister. "I didn't think I was gonna like orchestra music, but surprisingly, it wasn't half bad."

"Gee, thanks for that backhanded compliment, sis." Jasmine bumped Zoey with her elbow.

"Do you mind if I go over to congratulate Aubrey?" Jasmine asked her parents, but before they could answer, her boyfriend walked up.

"Hello, Mr. and Mrs. Lyndon." Case was carrying a small bouquet of red carnations.

"Good evening, Case." Mr. Lyndon shook his hand.

"Hi, Case," Mrs. Lyndon replied.

Case turned his attention to Jasmine. "These are for you." He handed her the flowers.

"Oh my God! Case, they're beautiful!" She handed her other bouquet to her sister and happily accepted the smaller bundle of carnations.

Mr. Lyndon shot his wife a look, but before he could say anything, she told Jasmine to go congratulate Aubrey. "We'll wait for you at the entrance."

"Aw, that was nice of her boo to come see her play." Zoey handed Jasmine's bouquet to her mom while she put on her coat.

"Yes, it was," her mom agreed.

"Did y'all see how quickly she tossed my flowers aside when he gave her that little raggedy bouquet?" Zoey's dad grumbled.

Zoey and her mom laughed.

Mrs. Lyndon slid the back of her hand down the side of her husband's cheek. "Now, don't you pout," she teased. "Jasmine appreciated your flowers too." She slid on her gloves. "And his flowers weren't raggedy. They were cute," she laughed.

A few minutes later, Jasmine returned with her bundle of carnations and a smile a mile wide.

"I'm ready!" she said.

"Let's go." Her dad placed his arm around her shoulder, and they headed home.

Chapter 8

Zoey's In A Funk

Over the next couple of days, things remained a little awkward between Zoey and her friends. The girls sat together at lunch, and although Olivia appeared to have made up with Tommi and tried to be the peacekeeper, the conversation still seemed forced. Zoey had been looking forward to Emily's sleepover, but now she wasn't sure if she even wanted to go.

On Friday after Zoey got home from school, she wanted to try and finish reading *Amari and the Night Brothers*. She nibbled some pretzels she brought from the kitchen as she sat in her comfy chair in the corner of her room.

Zoey's mom peeked her head in the doorway and asked, "What time do you want me to drop you off at Emily's?"

"Uh, I don't know," Zoey mumbled and turned her book face-down in her lap. "As long as I'm there by six o'clock, I guess."

Her mom tilted her head. "You sound like you don't want to go."

Zoey sighed. "I kind of don't."

"Hm. I thought you were looking forward to it."

"Honestly, I don't want to deal with Tommi," Zoey said. "She's been acting funky ever since she was caught lying about Josh. I just can't put up with any more of her drama."

Mrs. Lyndon sat at the bottom of Zoey's bed. "I know Emily would be disappointed if you didn't go," she said softly. "I understand you're upset with Tommi, but I think you should go anyway. Try putting this mess behind you. Go and have a good time. I wouldn't even bring up this business about her and Josh. You've been moping around the house for two days, and it's time to move on, kiddo."

Zoey thought about her mother's words for a moment. "You're right, Mom." She placed her book on her nightstand. "I don't want to disappoint my friends. I'll pack my things."

"Good girl! Let's plan on leaving at five-thirty." Mrs. Lyndon tapped Zoey on her foot and stood to leave.

"Oh, Mom! I forgot to ask if I could go with Olivia tomorrow morning to a basketball game at the community center."

"Since when do you like basketball?" her mom asked.

"I don't really. But Olivia's cousin is playing and one of our friends from school is on the team and asked if we'd come."

"What time tomorrow?"

"I think she said ten."

"I don't know, Zoey." Her mom placed her hand on her hip. "You're probably going to be tired. I'm sure you girls won't get much sleep tonight."

Zoey could tell her mom was not sold on the idea. "I'll be fine. I'll make sure I wrap my hair tonight so it will look nice in the morning. Olivia's mom will bring me home right after the game."

"Hm. Well, if you really want to go, I guess it'll be fine."

"Thanks, Mom!" Zoey smiled. "I'll text Olivia and let her know."

After Zoey texted her friend, she decided to focus on having a good time at Emily's. She wasn't going to bring up Josh at all. She grabbed her overnight bag from her closet and began packing. While she was packing her toiletries, her thoughts drifted to Grayson, and she realized she was actually looking forward to seeing him play basketball. She couldn't believe how easy it was to talk to him. And she couldn't believe he liked her. She found herself smiling when she thought of him.

Oh shoot! Does this mean I like him too? Zoey stuffed her toiletry case into her bag and then threw in a fresh pair of pajamas, her satin scarf to wrap her hair, a pair of gray leggings, and an oversized sweatshirt she'd wear to the game tomorrow. Now that her bag was packed, she tossed it on the floor and flopped across her bed to finish reading her book.

A few moments later, Zoey heard Jasmine yelling for her.

"I'm up here!" she called back.

Zoey could hear Jasmine running up the steps,

so she placed her book next to her and waited to see what her sister wanted.

"What time are you leaving?" Jasmine asked, leaning against the doorway.

"Not until five-thirty."

Jasmine sat at the bottom of the bed with one leg dangling off the side and the other tucked in front of her. "Listen. I know your girl Tommi has been acting real shady lately, but don't let her get to you."

"I already had this conversation with mom." Zoey gave her sister a lopsided smile.

"Cool! Because I don't want to have to jack nobody up. But you know I will if someone is messing with my little sis."

Zoey knew Jasmine was only playing and laughed at her silliness. "I promise, I'm good."

"I hope you have fun tonight, Zo!"

"I'm sure I will." Zoey smiled.

"What's that smile about?" Jasmine asked. "You look like you're up to something."

Zoey chuckled. "I was just thinking if I should tell you something or not?"

Jasmine leaned in and asked. "Wassup, Zo?"

"Grayson asked me to come see him play basketball." Zoey couldn't hold back her smile.

"Wait a minute! What?" Jasmine held up her hand. "Back up! When did this happen?"

Zoey laughed at her sister's theatrics. "He asked me when we were on the field trip."

"And you're just now telling me?" Jasmine pursed her lips together and shook her head in disbelief. "I can't believe you held onto that juicy tea for two whole days!"

"Sorry! I guess with all the Tommi and Josh drama—and then you had your concert that night too—I really didn't have time to tell you."

"I get it. You had a lot going on." Jasmine's voice was back to normal.

"Olivia and I are going to see him play tomorrow morning."

"Whoa!"

"I promise, I'll spill all the tea tomorrow when I come home."

"You better!" Jasmine gave her a hug before leaving.

Chapter 9

Time To Deal With
The Fallout

When Zoey arrived at Emily's house, Olivia and Tommi were already there. Zoey assumed they rode together since they live next door to one another.

"Zoey!" Emily and Olivia squealed as they ran to meet her at the door, almost knocking her over with their hugs.

Zoey giggled at their silliness and dropped her overnight bag at her feet so she could embrace them. She noticed Tommi gave her a slight wave, but her welcome lacked the exuberance of Emily and Olivia's.

"Now that everyone's here, we can sing karaoke." Emily dragged Zoey by the hand toward the door to the basement.

"But your cousin Jade isn't here yet," Zoey said.

"Oh, yeah! You did say she was supposed to be here," Olivia added.

"She sent me a text this morning and told me she was sick and wouldn't be able to make it." Emily flicked the light switch at the top of the basement stairs, and the girls bounded the stairs.

"Wow!" Zoey couldn't believe how spacious the basement was. "It looks like an apartment down here." There was a kitchen area with three bar stools in front of the counter island.

"They even have a movie theater room down here," Tommi boasted.

Olivia chuckled. "And don't forget about the popcorn machine."

"We can make some popcorn later if you want, but first, let's do karaoke." Emily turned on the strobe light, which rapidly flashed multicolored lights across the basement, then set up the karaoke machine. She selected the song she wanted to sing. Lizzo's "Special" started blaring out of the speakers a few seconds later.

Olivia, Tommi, and Zoey sang the background vocals. One of the walls in the basement was covered with mirrors, so the girls were able to see themselves as they performed. Zoey was glad Emily chose a song she already knew the words to.

Next, Tommi chose the song "24 K Magic" by Bruno Mars. The base from the music had the basement bumping and the flashing lights made it feel more like a party. The girls were pumped.

Zoey sang at the top of her lungs and let the beat of the music take her. No one seemed to care when they were off key or missed a word or two, all that mattered was they were having fun.

Once the song ended, Olivia fanned her face with her hand. "Can we turn on the air? It's hot down here."

"Yeah, I was thinking the same thing," Zoey said and removed her sweatshirt to reveal the ribbed tank top she wore underneath.

Emily flicked the switch to turn on the ceiling fans, then turned off the strobe light. "I'll turn the heat down a little bit." She turned the dial on the thermometer down a few degrees. "It should start to cool off in a minute."

"Thanks, Em," Olivia replied.

"Is anyone thirsty?" Emily asked as she walked to the kitchen area.

"I am." Zoey followed Emily to the refrigerator. "I can't believe you have an entire kitchen in your basement."

"Not really." Emily chuckled. "We don't have a stove down here. But it does come in handy when we have company."

Emily grabbed a bottle of water from the fridge, then handed one to Zoey.

"Hey! I'll take one of those," Olivia said as she sat on the arm of the sofa.

Emily picked up bottles for both Olivia and Tommi, then returned to her friends. The girls took a moment to catch their breath and enjoyed the ice-cold water.

Tommi sat in one of the swivel chairs and asked, "Can we talk?"

The girls shared a brief glance at one another, and Zoey hoped things wouldn't get awkward.

"Sure," they answered.

Tommi fidgeted with the cap on her water. "I need to apologize to all of you for how I handled this whole Josh thing. Especially to you, Zoey, because I was not honest with you when you asked me about him." Tommi paused for a moment before she continued. "I told my mom about what happened, and she helped me realize I wasn't being a good friend to any of you. And I'm sorry for being dishonest and not telling you guys the truth."

Zoey sat in the matching swivel chair and faced Tommi. "Why did you feel like you had to lie?"

"Honestly, I don't know." Tommi picked at the label on her water bottle. "When Josh and I first started talking, it was kind of fun not having anyone know we liked each other." She paused for a moment. "He wanted to tell you right away, and I didn't because I didn't want you to feel like I stole your friend."

"I never felt that way," Zoey replied.

"I can understand you not wanting to say anything at first, but we asked a couple of times if there was anything going on. And you continued to lie," Olivia said. "It was like you didn't trust us."

"I know! I messed up." Tommi leaned forward and rested her elbows on her knees. "Ever since the blow-up at the state capital, I've been miserable. If I could go back, I'd handle everything differently—but I can't. I just want to put this behind us and have my friends back."

Zoey felt like a weight had been lifted. They'd finally addressed the elephant in the room and could now move forward. Zoey stood and gave her bestie a big bear hug. Emily and Olivia joined in.

"Geesh! So glad that's over with. Now, you can tell us all about you and Josh," Olivia teased.

"Yeah, what's Josh like as a boyfriend?" Zoey sat again and used her tippy toes to swivel her chair side-to-side.

The girls were eager with anticipation.

Tommi dropped her head. "He broke up with me."

"What?" Zoey was shocked.

"Why'd he do that?" Emily asked, equally surprised.

"When did this happen?" Olivia asked.

Tommi shook her head. "He broke up with me on the bus ride home from our field trip." She paused. "He told me he felt like I was keeping our relationship a secret from our friends, and he didn't like it. And he really wasn't happy about seeing me with Bradley."

"What's the big deal about Bradley? He doesn't even live near us." Zoey asked.

"I understand why it bothered him. I mean, here I am hugging Bradley in front of all my friends. But I wouldn't hold hands with Josh because I didn't want anyone to know about us."

"Well, when you put it like that, I can see his point," Olivia said.

Emily nudged Olivia with her elbow.

"Ow!" Olivia rubbed her arm. "What'd you do that for?"

Emily narrowed her eyes and shook her head and couldn't believe how insensitive her friend was.

Tommi let out a soft sigh. "It's okay. Olivia's right. Now that I've had time to think about everything, I understand why Josh broke up with me." Tommi gave a half-hearted smile.

Zoey squeezed herself into Tommi's chair and hugged her neck. "I'm sorry he broke up with you."

Tommi let out a big laugh. "It's okay. We're still friends."

"Well, that's good news!" Zoey broke the hug but remained squeezed into the chair with her bestie.

"Yeah, that would have been awkward if you two weren't speaking," Emily agreed.

"Changing the subject. Guess who asked Zoey to come watch him play basketball tomorrow?" Olivia blurted.

"Wait! Did Grayson ask you to come see him play ball?" Tommi asked.

Zoey busted out laughing, and that was all the answer the girls needed.

"When did this happen?" Emily asked.

"Okay! Okay!" Zoey giggled. "He asked me on Wednesday when I was forced to sit with him, because somebody didn't save me a seat on the bus." Zoey gave Tommi a teasing look.

"Get back to the story. And I already apologized for that." Tommi smirked.

"There's nothing more to tell. He asked me if I'd come to see him play. He told me Olivia comes to their games sometimes to watch her cousin play.

I told him I'd come, and me and Olivia are gonna go tomorrow morning."

Emily's mouth hung open. "Uh, and you're only just now telling us?"

Zoey shrugged her shoulders. "After our fall-out, things were a little strained, so it just never came up. I did tell Olivia though, because I wanted to ask her about the games."

"You're forgiven. But make sure you send a group text tomorrow to let us know how it goes," Emily teased.

"Okay! I promise." Zoey chuckled.

The girls enjoyed spending this time together. They ate pizza, munched on popcorn, watched a movie, and talked until well after midnight. Emily's mother came downstairs around one o'clock and told them it was time to shut it down. She didn't want any of the parents mad at her because they stayed up all night. The girls continued to talk even after she turned off the lights, and one by one, they drifted off.

Chapter 10

Something New

The girls overslept the next morning, and Zoey and Olivia arrived late to Grayson's game. The first quarter was nearly over by the time they got there. They climbed the bleachers, following Olivia's dad to an empty row. Once they were seated, Zoey scanned the floor to see if Grayson was playing.

"There he is!" Olivia pointed at Grayson as he ran down the court.

"Don't point." Zoey smacked Olivia's hand down.

"Dang girl! It's not like he saw me," Olivia snapped.

"Let's just watch the game." Zoey didn't know the first thing about basketball, only that each basket was worth two points and occasionally three.

It didn't take long for Grayson to notice Zoey and Olivia in the stands. When he did, his face lit up.

"Oh! Did you see him smile at you?" Olivia whispered.

"Yes!" Zoey answered through clenched teeth as she smiled and waved at Grayson.

Zoey and Olivia talked through most of the game and cheered occasionally when Grayson or Olivia's cousin would make a basket. Zoey was surprised by how quickly it was over. She was glad she was able to come watch, but she was also tired and couldn't wait to get home.

After it ended, Olivia followed her dad to where her aunt and uncle waited for her cousin Thad.

Thad finally emerged from the dressing room and joined them. "Hey, cuz! Didn't think you were gonna make it today."

"Yeah, I went to a sleepover last night. But you know I'm still gonna support my favorite cousin."

"Girl, I'm your only cousin," Thad gave her a side hug.

"Yuck!" Olivia pulled away. "You know I don't like it when you hug me after playing ball," Olivia rolled her eyes. "You're all sweaty!"

Thad laughed and extended his hand to Zoey. "Hi. I'm Thad and this rude girl is my cousin."

"Nice to meet you." Zoey chuckled and shook his hand. Just then, someone tapped her on the shoulder.

When Zoey turned around, it was Grayson. He had apparently taken the time to towel down because he didn't look nearly as sweaty as Thad.

"Hey, thanks for coming." He stepped a little closer to her. "I was surprised when I looked up and saw you with Olivia."

"I told you I was gonna come." Zoey couldn't hide her smile. "By the way, congratulations to your team. You played a good game."

"Girl, do you even know anything about basketball?" He gave her a slight bump with his elbow.

Zoey laughed. "No! But I know you made a lot of baskets."

Grayson chuckled and stared at her for a moment. "Hey, I don't want to keep you, but is it okay if I text you later?"

Zoey's stomach was doing flip flops, and Olivia was staring at her smiling.

"Sure. That'll be fine."

"Cool!" He pulled his cellphone out of his duffle bag and handed it to Zoey. "Put your number in my phone, and I'll text you later."

Zoey took it and typed her name and number under his contacts, then handed it back to him.

Grayson's smile was so big it made Zoey smile too. *Hmm. How come I never noticed he has a dimple?*

"Hey, I gotta go, but I'll text you later." He gave her a parting smile, and then gave a quick bro-hug to Thad before leaving.

"Oh." Olivia hooked her arm through Zoey's. "Somebody wants to be your boyfriend."

"Girl, you're so crazy." Zoey laughed as she and Olivia walked arm in arm to their car.

Later that morning, Zoey was glad to finally be home. She was exhausted because they stayed up too late and then got up too early this morning, all she wanted to do was go back to sleep. But first she sat and talked with her mom and told her all about the sleepover and how grateful she was that she and Tommi had made up. Jasmine and her dad were at the grocery store, so she'd catch up with Jasmine later.

Zoey went up to her room to lie down and hoped she didn't fall asleep before Jasmine came home. She thought about how much fun she had with her friends last night and was happy she and Tommi were back to being besties. And when her thoughts drifted to Grayson, she smiled and thought to herself, *I don't know exactly what this is, but something is definitely happening. And I'm completely okay with that.*

The End

TEACHER'S GUIDE

Available at
everythingmicheal.com

Zoey Lyndon's Crush Chronicles

Please write a review

Authors love hearing from their readers!

Please let Micheal Anderson know what you thought of *Zoey Lyndon's Crush Chronicles*.

Leave a review on her website
everythingmicheal.com.

You can also leave a review on Amazon or Goodreads and this will help other children discover *Zoey Lyndon's Crush Chronicles*.

Thank You!

Micheal Anderson is an author who enjoys writing middle grade fiction and understands the value of representation in children's stories. She lives in St. Louis, Missouri with her husband and two daughters. Micheal enjoys blogging, jazz music and loves to travel abroad.

other books by Micheal Anderson

Printed in the USA
CPSIA information can be obtained
at www.ICGtesting.com
LVHW020419250124
769617LV00005B/705